HALF IN SHADE

D1571354

Half in Shade

FAMILY, PHOTOGRAPHY, AND FATE

Judith Kitchen

COFFEE HOUSE PRESS
MINNEAPOLIS 2012

Coffee House Press books are available to the trade through our primary distributor, Consortium Book Sales & Distribution, cbsd.com or (800) 283-3572. For personal orders, catalogs, or other information, write to: info@coffeehousepress.org.
Coffee House Press is a nonprofit literary publishing house. Support from private foundations, corporate giving programs, government programs, and generous individuals helps make the publication of our books possible. We gratefully acknowledge their support in detail in the back of this book.
Good books are brewing at coffeehousepress.org

LIBRARY OF CONGRESS CATALOGING-IN-PUBLICATION DATA
Kitchen, Judith.
Half in shade : family, photography, and fate / Judith Kitchen.
p. cm.
Includes bibliographical references.
ISBN 978-1-56689-296-4 (alk. paper)
1. Kitchen, Judith.
2. Authors, American—20th century—Biography.
I. Title.
PS3561.I845Z46 2012
813'.54—DC23
[B]
2011030609

FIRST EDITION | FIRST PRINTING

1 3 5 7 9 8 6 4 2

PRINTED IN THE UNITED STATES

For the past —
  where we came from

For the future —
  Benjamin, Simon, Ian

A Family Tree

(those mentioned or identified in photographs)

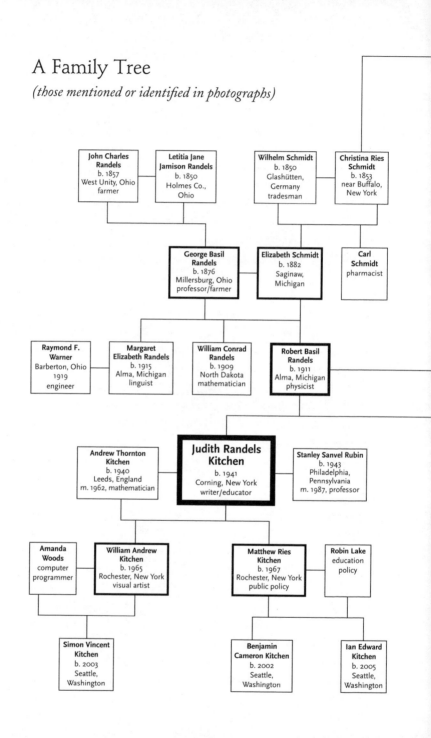

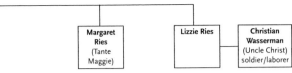

Margaret Ries (Tante Maggie)

Lizzie Ries

Christian Wasserman (Uncle Christ) soldier/laborer

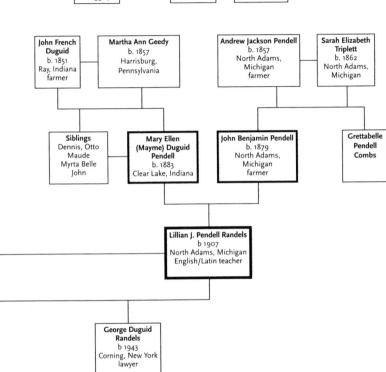

John French Duguid
b. 1851
Ray, Indiana
farmer

Martha Ann Geedy
b. 1857
Harrisburg, Pennsylvania

Andrew Jackson Pendell
b. 1857
North Adams, Michigan
farmer

Sarah Elizabeth Triplett
b. 1862
North Adams, Michigan

Siblings
Dennis, Otto
Maude
Myrta Belle
John

Mary Ellen (Mayme) Duguid Pendell
b. 1883
Clear Lake, Indiana

John Benjamin Pendell
b. 1879
North Adams, Michigan
farmer

Grettabelle Pendell Combs

Lillian J. Pendell Randels
b 1907
North Adams, Michigan
English/Latin teacher

George Duguid Randels
b 1943
Corning, New York
lawyer

Introduction

I HAVE NEVER OWNED A CAMERA and I never snap photos, except reluctantly when asked by others. I have always relied on memory to call up my personal images of the past. And so it was neither the curiosity of a photographer, nor some literary need to imagine visual images, that drew me to the haphazard collection of boxes and albums scattered on the bottom shelves, the ones my mother had managed to save from the floods. I don't remember anyone ever looking at them, and only later, when it was too late, did I wish I could question the photographers or their subjects. By then I realized I didn't know *who* they really were—these strangers we call family—lost now, slipping into the shade. But I wasn't done with them—or rather, they weren't done with me. Their stern faces kept turning in my direction, asking me to bring them back to light.

I found myself feeling grateful to those who had captured these earlier generations for me—the professionals who had posed them stiffly in their studios, and the amateurs who had caught them off guard in moments of frivolity. I became fascinated with the ghost in every photograph—the unseen presence behind the lens whose eye shapes what, and how, we will see.

A photograph sparks reverie and speculation. No two viewers will see it exactly the same way. There's something about the framing that makes us consider the presence—or absence—of an aesthetic. Snapshots, though, are somewhat exempt from artistic scrutiny. We note the composition, but we do not wonder about the use of negative space. Instead, we search out detail. Snapshots record a real, lived moment in time, lost the very second the shutter clicks.

As I sifted through the rough black scrapbook pages and the newer thin plastic inserts, I had no idea what I would find, or what I hoped to discover. Of course I did find the usual sepia portraits, and the perfunctory snapshots of reunions, first days of school, and summer vacations. But among the predictable photos, I also came across playful moments, oddball scenes, remnants of a past that felt oddly contemporary. I had begun to play detective, digging into my treasure trove for clues. Often, I had no way to identify the subjects, and no one I could ask. What, for example, drove my mother, Lillian, to make her way so far from the farm where she grew up? Who was she, before she became merely *my mother*? How did my Aunt Margaret actually see her scar? Who were those people who crossed the ocean to build a new country? How did someone else's family photographs appear, as if by magic, on my disk?

In an era of so many moving images, there is a mystery in the stilled moment. The very black-and-white of it. It serves as entry into another time, another place. I wanted my words to set things in motion. Suddenly—as a writer, not just as a viewer—I had a whole new set of questions. How to give "voice" to what is inherent in the visual? How to keep the visual from dominating, making all my thoughts redundant? I found myself experimenting with the placement of the photograph, investigating to see when—and how—the visual became integral and necessary. I used the snapshots as triggering devices, sometimes fixing on one, sometimes weaving them together, joining the generations, so to speak. I put people I'd never seen next to ones I knew intimately. I let them speak to each other, and to me.

My challenge as a writer was not to describe, but to interact. Not to confirm, but to animate and resurrect. The past became my subject, and memory my lens. But memory was often insufficient. In order to insinuate myself into the personal lives of others, I frequently had to rely on probability, supposition, intuition, the half known, the partially knowable. Sometimes out of desperation—or desire—I resorted to fantasy.

I became aware of a kind of triangulation: me, the photograph, and its subject(s). From my temporal advantage, I found I could supply what my subjects would never know—the future. I found myself in a kind of time warp in which I knew more *than* my subject, but less *about* my subject. My interest was not in uncovering a hidden narrative, or in enhancing a known story, or in revealing a specific character. I wanted to ponder how each individual life was/is framed by circumstance, how we are sometimes called to act, and sometimes merely to reflect.

In some way, snapshots are always retrospective. They take on new meanings as history unfolds. If it could be said that we measure time in wars—"Civil," "World," "Vietnam"—then we bring to any photograph the shadow of "before" or "after": Paris, 1938; Chicago, 1912; Edinburgh, 1964. Over and over, I found myself looking at faces that seemed so innocent. From my vantage in their future, I was able to sense what lay ahead of them. The older the photograph, the less I knew of its subject, but the more the photograph *and* subject seemed to step back in time, to fit itself into a larger, national history. I realized that, in many respects, the albums revealed patterns of American immigration and opportunities.

Then there were the words, also revelatory in their innocence: my grandfather's letters, my father's fragmentary memoir, my mother's journal, brief glimpses of someone else's life on the backs of postcards or envelopes, and identifying notations on the photographs themselves. Handwriting so individual and intimate that reality commanded pride of place. These people lived, and the sum of their lives points directly to the precarious present.

Half in Shade was written over a ten-year period. But it took a serious illness to make me realize that, like the people in the snapshots, none of us knows what lies beyond the moment, outside the frame. Each of the book's many sections is followed by a meditation on illness, as though to underscore our fragile ties. In writing about the uncertainties that had entered my own life, I came to understand that I was, in some way, taking my own photograph. Smile. Click. Okay, one more.

—Judith Kitchen

1.

Posterity will jump to conclusions:
that is its nature.

—JULIAN BARNES,
Flaubert's Parrot

The Speed of Light

The inner life of a human being is a vast and varied realm,
and does not concern itself alone with
stimulating arrangements of color, form, and design.

—EDWARD HOPPER

I SEEM TO BE STUCK in their wake, halting behind each of
them as they stop, pose, smile, then move apart, while I
wait patiently, then not so patiently, for them to finish. In
twenty-seven languages they speak the universal tongue—the
telltale *click* that says you're trapped in someone else's frame. The
place does not matter, though this time it is the Butchart
Gardens just outside Victoria, British Columbia. It's crowded,
and I can barely see the flowers for the people who stream past
them. In the distance, wild geese lift from the field where they
have been feeding, circle once, then settle in the farther distance
on a pond. The tractor that disturbed them drones on, turning
the earth for what looks to be yet another bed.

These are no ordinary flowers—or rather, they are ordinary
flowers set in extraordinary circumstance. Each individual garden tucks itself into the hillside, or wanders down to the water—
all but the regimental Italian garden that now occupies what was
once the tennis courts. The gardens swell with color: one all
white, from the tiniest rock creepers to the tallest hollyhocks;
another yellow and muted orange; and, of course, the subdued
greenery of the Japanese garden with its stylized miniature trees
and drab stone Buddhas, punctuated by one bright red bridge

over a studiously placid stream. By now the flowering trees have gone to green, and the rhododendrons are clearly past their prime. Today there's a riot of roses—those most boring of blooms, stiff on their thorny stems.

Stop. Position your subject. Raise the camera. Stop. Motion your subject to move a little to the left. There. Now you can see the roses too. *Click. Flash.* A document of your day. And there I am, pausing while you chatter away, oblivious, it seems, to anyone or anything else. Oblivious to the fine rain that falls, even as the sun insists itself, the day softened into the spectrum, all indigo and mauve. Or iris. Lilac. Lavender.

Rose.

My quick count tells me that two of every three people here are carrying a camera. Some carry two—one for the hand, another slung around the neck, zoom lens glaring like a ferret's eye. And there are camcorders as well, though roses do not dip and sway the way a field of tulips might, do not turn their heads or whisper or bow. So it must be all these milling, smiling people these cameras intend to seize—here on a Monday morning in mid-June, sometime in my past.

Among married couples, 92 percent of the time the man is in charge of the camera, but fairly often his wife wields a smaller version as well. Two women together either carry one each, or else none. In the amorphous groups of young people, everyone sports a leather case. Only children are free of the duty to record: they coil around lampposts, lean over the sides of fountains, poke or prod, race ahead or drag their heels—anything to disrupt the static posture of these planted beds, their planned finery.

What will the children remember of this day? The boredom. The see-through umbrella. The migrant feather found at the edge of the walk. The way Grandma kept stopping to sit on every bench. The way Uncle Martin made *them* stop so he could enforce his idea of family: Say *cheese, fromage, formaggio, queso, queijo, käse, kaas, chi-zu, jibini, tupi, serowy, ost.* In twenty-seven languages, smile.

I prefer their young memories—the inexplicable ennui—to the albums that will eventually shape this day in recollection, the fabricated family lined up against a background of fuchsias and pinks, backdrops to the drama of forced smiles and obligatory arms around shoulders.

In the photograph, we look *at;* the self becomes someone we watch with mild curiosity as the day spools out in three-by-five increments. The shutter *click*ed, and caught me thus, therefore I am.

In memory, we walk *through.* We reenact. We call up the slight shiver as the sun disappeared behind a cloud. We hear again the chatter, the mishmash of sounds as people call to each other, point and click. We conjure the moment when the wings all beat the air as if they were one large wing and the tractor made a syntax of sound. We stop to let the man ahead of us focus his third eye, as though he, too, would remember himself poised at the frozen edge of the moment before the moment before.

So, I hesitate just beyond the range of their future, a woman they did not notice or, when they did, they thanked politely as she halted her own passage through the day to make room for their documentation. What will they do with the stacks of prints tucked into their envelopes as though to preserve the limits of perception? The bottom drawers of twenty-seven countries grow steadily heavier, weighted with these self-defined memento vivere.

Photographers Anonymous. There must be a club for those who have sworn off this addiction, who *resist* the urge to snap and snag, whose memories provide the pigment, the sensation of the hand on the lizard-skin rail of the bridge, the goldfish wavering like coins in the water below. They meet in secret, in the pages of books, their ears attuned to what will make the eye respond, the inner eye, the one without the necessary attachments, where *zooming in* means going deep. They meet in secret, and they share their fear that we have lost the art of *seeing* to the technologies of *looking*. Look, they say, at what we've become. So many identical photographs—just lift out John and brush in Jacques. Same time, same place, same faces filled with stilted smiles. Same thoughts, same—oh, shame—desires.

"Return with us now to those thrilling days of yesteryear! From out of the past come the thundering hoofbeats of the great horse Silver," and I'm a child, sitting in front of the old Philco waiting for *The Lone Ranger,* 7:30 p.m., every Monday, Wednesday, and Friday, the voice on the radio conjuring the masked rider and his quiet companion, Tonto. I'm seeing it all unfold—the plains unrolling under Silver's hooves, giddy with sagebrush and tumbleweed, the mountains an austere blue in the distance. Where did I get that image—I, a child whose horizon was low-slung hills, a child who had yet to see a movie? Yet it was so clear, so perfectly mine.

And now I'm alive again in that time—maples shading the street like a dusk before dusk; the street itself cooling in that after-dinner hour when children can circle and circle on bikes, or prick their ears to the clanking refrain of kick-the-can; time held at bay until my mother's clear voice orbits the yards, calling us in to thrill to history.

Never mind that the speed-of-light hoofbeats were bathroom plungers pumped up and down in sand or gravel. Never mind that the gunshots were a cane slapping a leather cushion. Never mind that the rushing river was really crumpled paper. In my mind it was real, made all the more real because it happened only in my mind.

Imagination, then, must be the flip side of memory, not so much a calling up as a calling forth. Yet imagination also relies on knowledge: on knowing what is—and is not—possible in this world of fact. Imagination plants the seed or buries the bulb *knowing* the seasons will shift, seeing, in the mind's eye, April give way to August, the azalea to the rose, knowing that the red leaves of the maple will burnish in autumn, knowing that from this exact window, one can look down to the inlet where the moon's reflection will be just another shimmering white blossom.

And the photo? It catches the moon's reflection—here—held forever in this one impressionistic night, while the moon moves on, dropping below the horizon, giving way to the pastel dawn. While *we* move on to other gardens, other moments to record. The snapshot holds us still in our twenties, our thirties, our sixties. Past tense. Imagination fills the aperture, finds the griefs that caused the lines at the corners of the eyes. And memory reconstructs those griefs, faded now to bearable, but alive and squirming beneath the glossy surface, demanding their day in the brash, unflinching glare of the sun—the hidden ultraviolet damage of it—until grief cannot be glossed over, but finds us out again, and again.

This is not art. This is life, where grief accompanies our every loss, and every photo is a loss recorded. We sift through the album, grieving, even as we smile in recollection. In every language, it's a mixed blessing I stop for, waiting for strangers to complete the process so we can all walk on, in present tense.

Paris: 1938

SEPTEMBER EIGHTH, I know she was there. The evidence is inescapable. Someone named Rosa sketched her—one of those quick sketches by a sidewalk artist that almost, but not quite, catch your character. So in the drawing my aunt Margaret remains simply another young woman with short, bobbed hair, lips slightly too pronounced (more pronounced than in real life), eye with only the hint of eyebrow, oval of earring, characterless.

I don't blame the artist. Probably my aunt Margaret turned to her the one clear cheek, withholding everything that made her who she was. On the other, she had a scar, burned into soft flesh when as an infant she fell on the hot-air vent. A crosshatch scar that moved when she smiled. A beauty mark, though she probably didn't see it that way. What else didn't she see?

It was Paris, 1938. Innocence about to be assailed. *Time* magazine, September 19, 1938, along with ads for Robert Burns ten-cent cigars and Grace Line Caribbean Cruises, and following the "national" news that Roosevelt had pulled back slightly from a full alignment with Britain, gave an account of "foreign" news:

> Frenchmen were grimly convinced last week that Germany was in the very last stages of preparation for a war which Adolf Hitler would decide to fight now or later. . . . Heavy trucks rumbled into Paris and dumped sand at points where it would be handy to shovel into bags for

bomb shelters. . . . With wealthy families of Strasbourg already evacuating that border city, France, too, began to gird internally. . . . The Marseille stevedores, basing their stand on the French 40-Hour Week Law which the Cabinet took power to modify in special cases a fortnight ago, "Struck" by refusing to work over the weekends. . . . The nation sat tight to see if, after 19 years and ten months, the Armistice was about to end.

Heavy trucks were rumbling into Paris and my aunt Margaret was sitting on the small folding stool, her best profile turned toward a middle-aged woman—Rosa, her sign said—wearing black pants and a plain white shirt. This is the day she would keep. This day, like no other. The smell of the river, a mix of yeast and oil, and the first yellow leaves dropping to the pavement. The sun, absent behind skimming clouds, pale vestige of what it had been only a week or two before. The turn of the season, hint of what was coming. When this sketch was finished, she'd wander past the bookstalls, the peculiar smell of French books, like vinegar, and the sound of the language filling her with its liqueurs.

Families were leaving their homes in Strasbourg and my aunt Margaret was twenty-three years old, in Europe alone, drinking in everything she was about to lose. She'd given up her master's thesis on Bergson and Proust—the one her father had spent more time thinking about than she had. She'd given it over to her father's dream of what it might have become. Now she was searching for something new. She was on her own. There was more to this city than fusty philosophers and nostalgic old writers, an old man propped up in bed, longing for the past. There was energy in the air, movement, expectancy. Every word seemed to come to her with the clarity of fine wine, or woodsmoke. Rosa's hands moving so quickly, as though they had done this same sketch a thousand times, as though they would be there twenty years from this day. In the sketch, she would be beautiful, she just knew it.

Stevedores were striking in Marseille until their country called them to colors, and my aunt Margaret was trying to plan a future. There were no husbands waiting for a woman who seemed never to have heard of make-up, though the earrings suggest an attempt at dressing up. Or did Rosa simply add the earring, something to fill the negative space, something to draw the eye as it might in reality? The odds are fifty-fifty.

There are no odds on whether Margaret will stop at a café for coffee. Or whether she will buy a small book with a pale blue cover. Or whether she will keep the sounds of the language flowing through her, like a remembered river. Twenty-three, and alone. Paris, 1938.

Rosa stands back for a moment, then adds a straight diagonal line across the neck, as though to dress her subject in something simple, but elegant. With a flourish, she writes her name, and adds the date, the place: Boule Blanche, Montparnasse. The young woman smiles, and pulls out some notes. It's then that Rosa sees the other cheek. If only she'd known. She might have made art.

It's Paris, and the world should be opening to this young American. The world should be hers for the asking. In August, 1939, between ads for *The Saturday Evening Post,* air-conditioning, Florsheim shoes, the brand new Ford v-8, Goodyear's Double Eagle Airwheel tires that stop "4 to 223 feet quicker," Lucky Strike cigarettes, and portable victrolas, *Time* will publish a photo above the caption *gas-mask containers must not contain fishing tackle,* the accompanying text ominously flippant:

The face of lovely Paris is pocked with gun emplacements, searchlight batteries, and trenches. Recently a demonstration of air defenses was held in the ditched and tunneled Esplanade des Invalides outside Napoleon's tomb. . . . There are concrete gun platforms on the wooded Meudon and St. Cloud hills where Americans have their villas and restaurants serve cool drinks to heat-weary Parisians. . . . Large railroad station signs, a giveaway to low-flying raiders, have been removed. Seven of the main bridges leading across the Seine are being doubled and tripled in width to facilitate rapid evacuation. All Parisians whose work does not compel them to stay must leave the city for assigned villages when war breaks out. To avoid being billeted in barns the wise and wealthy have leased comfortable rustic retreats stocked with preserved food. If there is no war some families are going to become mighty tired of canned peaches.

Gas-mask containers must not contain fishing tackle? One sentence of semiexplanation: "Every Frenchman in Paris has his gas mask, and he is subject to fine if he uses its metal container to carry his fishing tackle." So they have imagined what ordinary men might do. But, despite Guernica, they have failed to imagine the future—Esplanade des Invalides, with its sandbag trenches, seems almost innocently ready for the last war, not the one to come.

What's the use of looking back? Trying to penetrate the sketch's static past? There is no one we can save. Rosa, given the nature of her work, will most likely become a collaborator. Or— and this we like to imagine—she will join the underground. One dark night, she will simply disappear. The bookstalls will close. Margaret will go home to America, although soon we could pick up her saga as a volunteer with the American Friends Service Committee in Ecuador and Guatemala. The scarred face of Esplanade des Invalides will be crosshatched with tunnels.

Ah, here's another photo: Margaret, 1948, sun in her hair, simple white blouse. Here she is, as I remember her. And then I see what I've been looking for: her left cheek—the one she deliberately turned to Rosa—with its distinctive flaw. So it was Rosa, then, glancing up, eyes back to the sketchbook then up again, who carefully disregarded what she saw, Rosa for whom fact was fiction. Margaret knew who she was all along.

Stop time, then, for the sake of imagination. Let Roosevelt stand behind Hull's statement that we are with France "in war as in peace." 1938. One day, like no other. Let the coffee be strong and uncommonly sweet. Let the sun record a sheen of rain on the rooftops, the afternoon winding down like a wind-up toy, the pigeons preening on the peaks, their three-note call—*je m'appelle, je m'appelle*—naming the present as though they had all the time in the world.

"With Cloud Chamber"

THIS IS WHAT A SCIENTIST should look like. The gooseneck lamp that twists in the direction of the glass rods that are somehow connected to the rubber tubes that are somehow connected to the drum into which my serious young father is peering casts long shadows in stripes over the ceiling and down the far wall. University of Michigan, 1939. His mind is ahead of his body, which waits and watches. This is a far cry from the computer screen, the digital world that turns fact into fiction, graphs and charts played out on the screen in multi-colored projections. This is the upshot of haphazard inquiry. Here things will whirl and whir and fill the space with sound—or else silence will tick away until, like magic, dials will pulse. He invents himself from shadow. His wrists reveal the short-sleeved shirt beneath his good black suit. The wires curl behind his ear, buzz with meaning. Surfaces glitter, see themselves in the glass, measure themselves against the rough wood of the frame. Jury-rigged—or jerry-built—that's what we'd say, but that would be later, after we knew his propensity for cobbling things together. After we sensed his love of the outmoded, the hopscotch world of tinkering. Careful. The arrow points to zero. Everything is about to begin.

"Robert, At About 3 Years Of Age"

THEY HAVE MANAGED to keep him clean to this minute, but it's clear he would defy geometry. Slide quicksilver past those two pairs of solid shoes, sideslip through the sluice of skirts, down the vertical axis and off into the garden before they can stand up, flustered, to call him back. He will return with a smudge of dirt on his shorts where he squatted at the edge of the flowerbed to watch a toad, a tear in the slip-stitched hem of his shirt that will cause them both to "ooh" and "oh" that his mother will be unhappy. And she will. Because she is always unhappy. And if he worried about that, he would have to suck in his smile and do what she wanted. If he were to give in to her dismay, he would not be able to catch that toad and hold it up to the light, the little pulse of a heart surging in its throat, its warty skin dry to the touch, and cool. He would have to stand there, starched and uncomfortable. He would be four. Then five. Then forever.

The white shirt tells him sit still, don't move. Above the collar, his hair is dark. It will not turn red for another year—and who knows why? Maybe because he loves the feeling of not knowing, of wondering what, and why, and how. He loves these two old women—his grandmother and her sister, Tante Maggie—whose stern faces unwrinkle in his presence. He loves the plain lines of their lives that lead directly to his. He thinks they are one, and they are his. It is 1914. They come from somewhere in the century before, when life was a thing to be harnessed and contained. Between them, they have many years of age, many years of moving between German and English, their accents caught between there and here: 484 (even the house number is symmetrical) Somewhere Street, Saginaw, Michigan. Or is it St. Louis? He could have told me. Could have said what it is to escape the isoceles to discover where these parallel lines might intersect. But for now, for this brief moment in someone's sun, he is the good one who comes when they call, filled with the small adventures they have permitted him: grass, toad, the ironed scent of sunshine, the soft, burred sound of his name.

Circa 1873

ORN BEFORE THE CIVIL WAR into another language. They looked out at everyone with the same burning eyes. No one thought of one without the other, though the one with the light ribbon at her neck lived long enough to count my toes in German.

They were born before the Civil War, but it touched them with troubled fingers. Their younger sister, Lizzie, married a man who had seen Shiloh. Chickamauga. She married his haunted footsteps and his God-fearing love of pageantry.

They were born before the Civil War, so the one who will be my great-grandmother watches us now with something that resembles compassion. As though they can already guess what we still have to learn, these fastidious sisters of circumstance.

Great-Uncle Carl

HOW DID HE EVER get to be somebody's uncle? Here he is, sitting like any good six-month-old, facing the huge black box with its one prying eye. His christening dress covers his tiny clubfoot so here you can't tell that he'll never walk right. Stoic, he stands up well to our collective scrutiny, fends off intrusion with his steady reciprocal stare.

Double Exposure

after Stuart Dybek

"**M**Y BROTHER is the young man on right of this picture in a store in Chicago after leaving the McIntyre store in St. Louis." My grandmother's scrawl—so familiar, so unexpected, given her diminutive size and her excessive gentility—runs haphazardly down the back of the photo and there he is, dapper in his gleaming white shirt and suspenders, leaning against the counter staring into the glare of the treeless street.

No one would know, this far in the future, that somewhere hidden by the plane of the ice cream table—the one with the glass filled with straws—his clubfoot rests at an awkward angle. All around him, sun rubs a sheen on the curves of the bentwood chairs. Behind him, it glances off the tin ceiling and strokes the glass doors of the phone booths. Two women are seated beneath a Bell sign, and one—it's hard to tell—seems to be speaking into a mouthpiece. The man on the left, the obvious owner, reiterates his mustache with bow tie and watch chain. The electric fan purrs. What kind of store is this, cigars in one case, jars in another . . . and look, a ladder that leads to that neat row of hundreds of labeled bottles? They must hold powders or tinctures, to be meted out in small doses. Drugstore. Chicago, circa 1912.

The black-haired woman waits for something to happen. She shifts in her chair and repeats herself in the glass like a muted refrain. Ghostlike behind her/before her, another young man takes a quick look into the window, hesitates as though he could enter the half shade and find refreshment. But he is leaving Chicago. Leaving its swelter and vague disappointment. From here, he will cross to the alley and make his way under the elevated tracks casting their lattice of shadows. He will move beyond the neighborhood, winding his way toward the river, caught in a story of someone else's making.

The year will turn and most men his age will begin to imagine the hard fields of France. But not Uncle Carl, who will limp home after standing all day, measuring and mixing. And not the unknown young man who by now has forgotten his dim room above the bar and followed the river like a woman's laugh through the darkened streets of the city. Soon he will appear on the shore of a lake so wide it could easily be the ocean. Standing there, the shimmering white face of a black-haired woman will float at the edge of his dreams. Soon, very soon, he will take off his trousers and his glowing shirt and tie, fold them neatly next to his oddly warped shoes, dip his toes into the cold, and disappear below the surface of the page.

Where They Came From,
Where They Went

I'D LIKE TO THINK they belong to me—or I to them—this young couple who appear to be on shipboard. Young, and healthy, and staring into the sun. Staring westward, I imagine, looking toward that moment they will land in the country of their dreams. It's the mid-1800s, maybe, and they will make their way to Buffalo, New York, then on to Michigan where my grandmother will be born. I'd like to think they were mine—and by all rights they should be, handed to me (as they have been) by the woman in the photography shop, the woman who carefully handled and sorted my family, scanned their brief histories into the machine that put them on a disk where I now hold their thin metallic future. But when I sorted through the originals looking for handwriting on the backs, terse identifications of the people I've never met, I could not find this one. And I don't remember giving it to the proprietor, I don't remember seeing it, ever. Somehow this couple has made their way—insinuated themselves—into my family lore, raising their glasses with the rest of them to what I may (or may not) find of the lives they actually led.

So here they are, my (theoretical) great-grandparents, so different from the stiff faces that stared down from their perch in the front hallway of my childhood. Here they are, wind in their hair, and something else—a readiness in their faces that I don't recall as part of my heritage. Just look at the way she squints her half smile while he stares, shadowed, into the lens. Just look at the way the wind lifts her scarf and curls around her like a purring cat. I like to think, by the half-seen elbow in the background, that behind him someone is playing the harmonica. That the song, too, coils in the wind, but not before he has heard its eager call.

They've left the old life behind—the one they might have led if they'd stayed—and now they are suspended between what they know and what I now know better than they ever could. Between what they might have thought they could be and what they eventually became. From this moment on, they will pose for those others, the ones in the old country whose spidery letters recount people and places they will never see again. Just as their own rough handwriting will spill out opportunity—a clapboard house, a mill, two children who retain a smattering of German even as they skip off to school. Or rather, in the case of their son Carl, limp off to school in the special shoe the cobbler made for his clubfoot, the shoe that twisted his twisted bones back toward the true—at least enough to get him to school and, later, to walk him every day to the drugstore where he worked an entire life.

Carl would have been the age of my grandmother's other cousin Karl—the one in that other life—who posed somewhere in Glashütten, Bavaria, with his wife and son in 1937. There is the old garden—the one they might have had—with a lace-covered table and a decanter of sherry, at least it looks like sherry, but the glasses are too large (and too full) for it to be sherry. So wine. And only two glasses for three people, so we assume this is for the two men. Some occasion. Look, her right hand holds a blossom in her lap and her left hand covers something—a box? Who knows? Look again, there's something on the table, in the foreground— a ribbon of some sort, crimped at the edges, shaped like a sun. How prim and proper it all looks, staged, and how impossible to freeze the forced smiles, to hold so stiff and still.

What will happen to them all? From the crimped filigree of German script on the back, it's hard to decide if cousin Karl's son is called Friedrich or Wilhelm. And what will it matter in a few short years when he will be called nothing at all, when there will be no one to call him? If he comes back, he will come back to a diminished thing: a garden unkempt, a broken wall. If he comes back, he will come with all he has seen clouding his eyes, carrying that lockstep method he's learned to look away. If the camera catches him, it will catch the phantom of the man he might have been, staring emptily into a garden gone to seed.

But today—the day of the open shutter, the window open to this infusion of light—they have no way of knowing that they are caught between the white flare of the filigreed cloth and the flash of the Allied bombs that will shatter their world. They smile and raise their glasses. The flowers in the vase release the familiar scent of home. The mother wears her Sunday best. On this side of the ocean, our Carl makes his halting way to the drugstore, fills his glass with Coca-Cola, speaks to the customers, counts out change.

Friedrich (or is it Wilhelm?) looks to be about the same age as Carl's sister Elizabeth's son—the young man studying physics at the university who will soon become my father, the young man who wears his pacifism on his sleeve so that it ages with him. He will not go off to the war that is calling, and perhaps it is because he senses Wilhelm (or is it Friedrich?) stiff in his garden pose. Has seen the faded letters that attest to another life. And that's the point, that there is life.

Maybe it's simpler than that. Maybe it's the year he was fifteen when he and his family lived in Freiburg while his father was on sabbatical, the gymnasium Robert attended—all those boys his own age, Otto and Heinrich and Johann. Maybe their faces swim before him, still fifteen, still his boyhood friends.

That was the year my grandfather wrote a postcard to someone—but who?—describing Munich. "This card tells its own story," he says, then asks, "Does the city look as it did 40 years ago?" After a disquisition on the city's churches, he closes with "I am not the man in the baloon [sic]" and signs it, simply, "George." There's a teasing intimacy there, and more. A surprising ignorance. One is tempted to say a "willed ignorance," but who among us recognizes the future breathing down our necks?

Maybe my father will be disillusioned when he returns, fifty years later, to learn how many of his boyhood friends went off willingly to war. Maybe he will wonder why his face did not come to mind. (I say maybe, then add maybe to maybe, because his, too, is now a face from the past, and these are at best conjectures, attempts at correlation.) For the moment of my speculation, though, my twenty-something father-yet-to-be is unwilling. And he is innocent in the way that only an American can be innocent. He allows himself that innocence.

It's the same innocence you see on the faces of the sunlit strangers on my disk. The ones I've borrowed, briefly, and imbued with basic facts. So look again. Put a hat on Wilhelm, or Friedrich, take him out of his garden and place him on deck. Cover his hair and you suddenly see that unknown immigrant: the same flinty back, ramrod tie, strict mouth beneath the softer eyes. Can we simply chalk that up to coincidence? Or do we have to concede the less than scientific, the more than uncanny, the serendipitous?

Now I wonder where those strangers came from, where they went, that they could come ashore in twenty-first-century technology, land in the midst of my family stories with such a look of expectation. What were their real lives? All the maybes hurl themselves at me. Let's say they made it to Montana, where the memory of old gardens disappeared into the width of sky, but then the farmland withered in the drought. Their daughter's daughter married and moved on, as far north and west as she could go and still remain American. Their son Henry drifted into alcohol, even before his son, Hank, was called up—1943. On August 19, 1944, somewhere in France, Hank came face to face with a young German soldier, a boy so like him he might have been staring into the wavery mirror in his grandparents' hallway back in Butte. Let's say Hank went in my father's stead. Who lost his name that day at the Battle of Chambois? Which young man came home? All these lives, making a recombinant DNA of history.

Ten years later, in the surging uncertainties of the fifties, my father took us to Wyoming, where we camped and canoed and learned to climb mountains. We were instructed in how to place the piton, how to scale a sheer rock wall and find a toehold. How to rappel. We learned to lower ourselves over the ledge, trusting the rope—and our own sheer will—to keep us safe. My mother stayed below while my father showed us how to face down fear. The camera holds him there, backlit, balanced between earth and sky, doing what even those two daring strangers could never imagine, carrying their fortitude forward—or away—whichever you choose to call it.

Bits and Pieces: 1

fragments of an incomplete memoir by Robert B. Randels

THE WAR HYSTERIA OVERTOOK Alma in 1917 just as it did nearly every other city in the country. German-Americans, whether alien or citizen, were closely watched by their neighbors and sometimes even by the authorities. At the college, the male students rushed out to form a Student Officer Corps, kind of an ad-hoc ROTC, and a uniformed army man joined the faculty to train officers. The campus army set up headquarters in Hood Museum and the football field became a parade ground. Between classes they marched and countermarched, double-quick marched and wheeled; they counted off and went through the manual of arms with broomsticks for guns. We six-year-olds were a loyal cheering section and would creep up as close as we dared to the impenetrable phalanx to marvel at the endurance shown by these recruits.

But since war is not all parades and inspections, the officers-to-be must have some training in trench warfare. Therefore a pair of trenches were dug in the lawn near the tennis courts, each about eight feet deep and twenty or so feet long. There was a shelf at the four-foot depth on which a recruit could stand to aim his broomstick at the opposing trench. When filled with trainees, each trench held about a dozen men and at the command "over the top" they'd scramble out into "no man's land," wiggle like snakes toward the opposite trench where they made spearing motions toward its occupants. They never seemed to choose up sides and really act like Americans and "Huns" the way we children did when playing cowboys and Indians, so their imitation of our game was really quite tame.

The trenches had been dug into a clay knob. The moraines and glacial alluvium of the Pine River valley provided interesting contrasts in the soil and subsoil constitution of neighboring lots. A real clay knob was sticky as glue in spring, hard as rock in summer, and whenever moistened slightly by a shower, slick as grease. It was after a shower when several of us decided that our children's war games should be moved to more realistic surroundings, say out in the trenches. We varied in size from about three and a half to four feet tall, and also in strength and agility. The earlier spring rains had filled the lower part of the trench with muddy water almost even with the marksman's platform. It was easy to slide down into the trench but quite a scramble to get out again, requiring a boost from below and it helped a lot to have a tug from above. Four of us were playing but suddenly there were only three, for Harry Means had slipped into the deep part of the trench. You couldn't see anything in that muddy water till his head bobbed up. Bill McCurdy reached over and grabbed his hair and pulled him ashore where Leo and I helped drag him onto the shelf. We pushed and pulled each other out of the trench and went into a closed meeting to discuss the story we'd give our respective parents. . . . I don't know whether it was the scare of almost losing a playmate or the fear of consequences of coming home with muddy clothes, but anyway, we stopped playing trench warfare. Even the college men played with less enthusiasm, the whole idea of officer training was beginning to pall and when, in November, 1918, the trenches were quietly filled with dirt, War itself was buried in them.

Plaid

I'LL START WITH MY FATHER, 1937, newly married, wrapped in the wool blanket my mother bought when she took a tour of Europe. I'll start with his pleased satisfaction, the dashing way he cocks his hat. Who could resist a redheaded man willing to drape himself in red? The shadows of shadows sweep down at the same acute angle until every dimension is the square root of the sum of the square of its sides. Roofline and wagon. Chinline, clothesline, and even his fancy white shoes.

Look how his stance mirrors his mother's, though she is not yet his mother, not here, with the century newly beginning.

Here she is simply Elizabeth, her marriage newly beginning. 1906. Somewhere in Europe, probably Germany, impossible to tell. *"On nearly every hill there is something of note perhaps some old castle in ruins, or the remnants of a tower built in the tenth or eleventh centuries. It makes one feel distinctly that there has been a past. We make long tours to see these old stone walls but there is something more interesting about them than stone and mortar. One can appreciate better the manner of life here in the middle ages. We walked as much as 20 miles one day to see an old tower."*

She's wearing a rain hat (or so it appears—it glints in the half light) and good solid boots that lace up her calves. She's solid no-nonsense, no frills.

Half in and half out of her life in front of an overcast cottage, she appears to be headed for more than she got. Appears to be looking for more than the teas and the doilies that made up the frugal habits that defined her. I recognize something that some-day I'll have to resist.

But now that they're dead, here they are—years apart, but peas in a pod—criss-crossing each other's paths. And mine. Ancestors stilled to their essence. Though nothing is still. The wind picks up; the clock unwinds; time sweeps its clean passage through all the loose ends. And I'm left with sheer speculation: what she did or didn't give him, what he might or might not have refused to take.

The cottage behind her, with its half-thatched roof, its shaded interior—what might have happened to it? We have the advantage of hindsight; we know about war and its aftermath. But who ever knows what will crumble and what will endure? Maybe we could locate that house, find its global position and see it standing, intact, one intrepid foot planted firmly in the future, squaring its shoulders against the fleeting past.

Notebook

—GEORGE B. RANDELS, 1906

Illustration which might be used in commenting on nature of authority & commanding:
Verboten *in Germany a most common word. People without any questioning obey as if it came from a higher & unquestionable source. Everywhere along the R. R. it is found. The last little stretch of R. R. had its* verboten *but coupled with its reason: it is dangerous to put the head out of the window. Here for the first time did we see the* verboten *transgressed. It was very natural too. The moral one had to draw was that a comment loses its very essence & much of its effectiveness when accompanied by reasons for issuing the same. It becomes only advice.*

Bits and Pieces: 2

fragments of an incomplete memoir by Robert B. Randels

ONE OF THE CASUALTIES of the first war was a professor at Alma. Professor Dr. Bober was a very correct, courteous, even courtly gentleman, born in East Prussia and educated in Germany. Any school should have been happy to expose its students to his teaching of German language and literature, for his perfection of speech and manner was fit to be learned and even copied. In the interest of protecting the country from internal subversion and to save democracy, the government placed restrictions on the movements of "enemy aliens." In the first decades of the century most immigrants took out so-called "first papers," and this was considered by nearly everyone to constitute naturalization, but in 1917 people with German names and only first papers became "enemy aliens" even though they might have sons fighting in the u.s. Army in France, often aiming across the trenches at their cousins. This was the case in the Bober family, but Dr. Bober could walk no more than five blocks from the college campus on pain of arrest and there were plenty of 110% Americans ready to do just that. He accepted the indignity with stoic calm but it must have hurt deeply to have always to trust the mailing of a letter to his son or to a student courier since his "radius" prevented his reaching the post office. Dr. Bober was subjected to catcalls and jeers and on one occasion a mob formed. The dean arrived in time to prevent the threatened violence.

Classroom with Landscape

THIS IS PERHAPS THE ONLY TIME I've seen her with short hair, so she looks foreign to me, even as she is so clearly herself. She's eleven. 1927. The school is somewhere in Freiburg im Breisgau where her father is spending his sabbatical. Dead center—maybe they placed her there for the class photograph, their American guest—she stares straight through me in my own language.

Twenty-five girls, arranged in tiers, some standing on benches behind, and then, behind them—a landscape, off-center, the only decoration on the wall. You can barely make out trees, a river reflecting the light. Which one of the others is Martha, the friend who will become the opera singer? She could be any of them, I think, with their long blond braids, their big-boned capacities. So let her be sitting next to my aunt Margaret wearing a checkered jumper and a half smile.

Maybe it's the end of the year, and Margaret can hold her own in German. There's a book open on her desk, as though she has mastered the whole of what it took eleven years in English to accomplish.

Let it be April, the sun springing to life, her brothers planning their long trek through Scotland, and Margaret herself thinking of how she has just turned twelve, will soon become a teenager somewhere far away, in Michigan. She will keep Martha as her friend, she knows she will, because she wills it thus. She folds this year inside her, like the handkerchief she has learned to keep in her pocket. She folds it in, like whipped egg white, so imperceptible it simply lightens the batter. And then she walks home.

Already it is growing in her—the life she has yet to lead, and the death she has yet to face. Locked in her ovary—the one that has not yet released one egg—is the shadow of the cancer that will kill her. On the way home from school, she thinks of what she will tell her mother. *Today they came to take a photograph. I sat next to Martha. I wished for long blond hair and braids. Do we need to go home? I've forgotten everyone I ever knew there. I've forgotten the English words for the stories I make up in my head.*

It will be August when the family is photographed with Loch Lomond behind them. A strange, austere group, dwarfed by water and mountain and most of all, sky. Four of them, on a tiny spit of land, sentenced to their lights and darks. Her father, her mother, her brother Robert in knickers, fifteen years old. Her oldest brother, William, must have taken the shot. There's no one else in sight. To their right, there's a hint of a roof—something that glints in the sun, at a slant. The family faces forward, their reflections rippling beneath them. There's another shot of Robert standing in front of a stone wall, the loch lost in a landscape so bleak it makes her feel lonely. Over his shoulders, bald mountains bleed into the absolute gray of the sky.

She will feel small again, in the presence of her two older brothers. She will feel the lake stretch out at her back, hiding the monster she imagines in its depths. It will be August, in another country, and Margaret will be dreaming still in German, holding it close to her heart so that, when she goes home, she can write her friend Martha a letter as though they were not already drifting apart.

———

And then it will be July, eleven years later, and Margaret will open the envelope to Martha's wedding photograph. She smiles out at her as though no time at all has passed. It's clear, isn't it? The camera does not lie. Martha does not know; her unnamed husband does not know; the photographer—someone named Koch, Salzstrasse 13, Telefon 6382—does not know. Juni, 1938. But they must all suspect. Only four months to go until that

infamous night of broken glass. But this is young love. They need flowers, and music. They need to turn their backs and dance. Who knows what will happen? Who can imagine that one day two middle-aged women will become long-lost friends, briefly reunited, after all the history they could not see coming as they sat there under the shining river, shyly conjugating their steadfast verbs?

Time and Tide: Five Letters

Alma, Michigan, 1936

Dear Margaret,

After you left I thought of the fact that you will need to be in the Hope Church on Sunday so will need to modify your plans for the weekend in Grand Haven to that extent.

To try to grasp firmly Bergson's use of Time: Here is a quotation from a commentator on Bergson's philosophy. "The principle then of this philosophy is that reality is time, that it can be expressed in terms of time, that it is the very stuff of which consciousness and life are made."

If you repeat this 1,000 times (here times is not used in Bergson's way) you will begin to believe it, and it will seem just as natural as to say anything else is real like matter. We have talked so much about matter that we have got to thinking it is something real, and it is likely there isn't as good grounds for that belief as there is for thinking "time" is real.

Your father

Dear Margaret,

Count the Schmidts as they go by. There were 49 when we visited Langensteinbach. Take a yardstick and cut a notch in for each of your second, third, and more remote cousins. Probably one yardstick would not suffice. You may entertain some of them at least at my expense (I am hedging a little, don't take them all.) Maybe you could have Lydia and her family or maybe some cousins she is more intimate with in to dinner at the Inn. I want you to do something a bit extra for Lydia. . . . We will want to be remembered to the various Karls, Wilhelms, Friedrichs and Phillips and the feminines of these names.

The German boat made a nice transition from America both literally and as a preliminary approach to the language. Are you in Nürnberg today? There I learned what "umsonst" meant. On Saturday we visited the St. Sebaldus church. An Eintrit fee was expected. I told the attendant that I guessed I would wait till the next day to visit the church. Her caustic remark was that I wanted to visit it "umsonst." [free] I thanked her for what I supposed was a compliment on my church-going proclivities. Later I sensed the meaning of the language.

Tomorrow Mama and I celebrate our 32nd wedding anniversary.

Your father

Alma, November 12, 1939

Dear Margaret,

It is alright to keep the car till Thanksgiving. I accumulate some change in my pocketbook when there is no car to feed. I get a little exercise. I walked out to the farm early enough to ride back with Mr. Grandy who starts work at 6 a.m. at the sugar factory. I don't mind the walk in the least, for the weather and roads were both nice. I think this is going to be a nice day so maybe you will use the car.

I have no report yet from Robert as to the outcome of his Prelims. I expect he will be writing about the results soon and I expect them to be favorable. But then one can not be sure of such things.

The college is having some disciplinary problems, drinking mainly, some (2) expulsions, but mainly first offenders, so far as college knowledge goes at least . . . I think Miss Gillard is making the mistake of believing all rumors of evil and inviting tale bearing. I shall not be surprised if she is in for an uncomfortable time.

I presume Mrs. Ver Hey is excited about the headlines these days. I am making no prophecies although I don't think it likely the Germans will attack the Netherlands. Several reports I have seen from Amsterdam said that much of this talk was from the English who were trying to stir up more feeling among the Hollanders against the Germans. I hope there isn't anything more to it.

We lost another football game. Maybe we haven't as good a team as I thought for.

Your father

July 4, 1940

Dear Margaret,

Have just returned from the haying field. The thing that makes me mad is to hear a plane above wasting gasoline for defense while below in a hay field working is one able bodied man, two junior high school girls, and an old college professor of about 65 years of age. This is all so the cows will have hay next winter to give milk to raise cream to make butter so the English have butter & cheese to fight the Germans and to make the world safe for bolshevism. (Of course I am not so bitter against the bolshevists as most of their supporters are.)

. . . This is early the Fourth of July. We have our flag out but can not remember with certainty the grammar of flag hanging practice.

Your father

Dear Margaret,

I am glad you had an opportunity to make the acquaintance of Mr. Robert Frost and to know his daughter. I think Mr. Frost is my favorite of the living poets. You will have a chance to see Vermont stone fences, the setting of "Mending a Fence." I suspect the inner reality of the poem can be realized in mending a Michigan fence although a barbed wire fence is not nearly so poetic a setting. The barbs are suggestive of the tempers which usually go with a line fence. I think even I might be more considerate with my neighbor if the fences were stone instead of barbed wire. But I imagine that even stone fences are exasperating—the stones probably do not stay readily where put, and they may bruise one's finger. Maybe it depends more on the disposition of the neighbors.

Your father

"Rain Coming from a Bright Sky" *

THIS MOMENT, so unexpected, so out of the norm. And Karl, playing around with the rest of them. She wishes she'd worn her blue blouse, the one that goes with her eyes. But how could she expect him to notice her, with Elsa and Malena so trim and pretty even in these awful shoes? If only her hair would stay in place and she had a bit more bust. Still, she thinks, when he smiles at her the day lights up—like that afternoon last May when a rainbow threw its arch across the valley and everything looked vivid in its rinse of color. A day like that is something to cherish, the sky so washed and innocent.

This could be any occasion anywhere—such rollicking fun, accordion-filled. This could be from any family album, singing out its era as they sing along. Can we see anything in these faces to help us understand? Stripped of those uniforms, couldn't they be us? Brought to light in October 2007, they run down that bridge—there—square in the middle of 1940s Poland. Maybe, if we only knew enough, we could break down the film's defenses, penetrate the moment with a burst of comprehension. They do not see us coming as they turn their backs and dance within their formal fluted borders. And isn't that what the nature of the snapshot—its moment trapped in time—underscores? So it's context that determines how we'll read them. Unearthed from attics and cellars, they are once more called to order, once more facing us with (*we could never . . .*) what they were. Look at them locked in that shining flashbulb instant. Look at us fending off its blinding glare.

* The photograph in this essay is part of a European collection found in 2007, now archived at the United States Holocaust Memorial Museum in an album entitled *Auschwitz through the lens of the SS: Photos of Nazi leadership at the camp*. Its description reads: "Nazi officers and female auxiliaries (Helferinnen) run down a wooden bridge in Solahütte. Karl Hoecker is pictured in the center. The original caption reads 'rain coming from a bright sky' (figuratively 'something unexpected')."

Bits and Pieces: 3

fragments of an incomplete memoir by Robert B. Randels

ALTHOUGH MY NAME gave no hint of my mother's German heritage, I was marked by some Sunday School classmates as a "Boche" since I could speak some German. My parents had thought it a good idea to bring the children up bilingual and it did help when we stayed with our grandparents, for even what passed with them as English had a liberal admixture of German words almost like the so-called Pennsylvania Dutch. My bilingual nature abruptly changed to mono one Sunday morning when I used a German word at the wrong time and a classmate decided to knock it back down my throat. The resultant nosebleed spelled the end of a perfect German accent for I didn't speak German again for eight years.

But the real problem was yet to come. My father's great fat Webster's Unabridged had several color plates of birds, flowers, architectural styles and, on one page, the flags of all nations. Each color plate had tissue paper to prevent the transfer of printers' ink onto the slick color pages. The tissue being transparent, the flags could be traced and colored with crayons, the entire page could be easily reproduced. For some reason, I enjoyed this exercise—similar projects came home frequently from the College library in the pages of a magazine—*Normal Instructor and Primary Plan* I think was the name—and I had a complete set of flags of my own, including a German flag. I told my playmates that I had a German flag and the word got around the neighborhood.

One evening quite a gathering of neighbors and some from quite a distance formed under the street light on the corner so my father went out to see what was up. He soon found out, for the mob wanted my German flag and if it was not given up, were prepared to paint the house yellow. When real or imagined enemies had their houses painted yellow by such mobs, the attention was more to the general effect rather than thoroughness in coating all the wood that faced the weather. In any case my father argued that he knew of no German flag although he could see nothing particularly wrong in having one if he wanted it. The mob's persistence was such that I was summoned and asked what I knew about it, so I went to the Dictionary and brought the page out. I proceeded to identify and name about twenty flags as the basically friendly neighbors slunk off toward home.

I think the flag bit was only a trigger. I suspect that many thought my father was a slacker, avoiding his duty to his country. As a young man, I had assumed that he had been a conscientious objector, opposed to killing, if not on religious then on philosophical grounds. It was almost time for the next war when I learned that he had volunteered early, probably in May of 1917. He thought that his special knowledge of Psychological Tests and Measurements would be helpful; he believed in Mr. Wilson and shouldn't the "world be made safe for Democracy"? But the Sanitary Corps (for that was the group in the army assigned to do psychological testing) found that he had a slight hernia and couldn't accept him unless he had an operation. Such a flimsy excuse persuaded him that the Corps didn't really want him and he always had a fear of surgeons' knives. I've often thought that we as a nation missed a good bet for he would surely have come up with "Army Gamma" to go with the Alpha and Beta which were used during and after World War I. In my imagination it would be a test given only to officers to test their fitness to lead, based on the premise that "War is too serious a business to be left to the Generals." It would have picked out philosophers for the high command.

Standard Time

W E'VE STOPPED SAVING DAYLIGHT. Now, in the dark diminished hour of five o'clock, light hovers somewhere over the water, a second horizon floating above the first, bright for a lingering moment, then gone. It comes again in early morning—earlier morning—when we don't yet want to be awake. Oh we know that it helped our grandparents on the farm, helped them milk and feed in the milklight of a November sunrise, but we have left all that behind.

Daylight. Day delight. The calypso of four years old, early to rise into the dawn. The wide expanse of lawn where the conscientious objectors planted their long rows of lettuce. More than a victory garden: feeding the war, but not fighting it. Scud and scuffle of hoes, my father showing them how to lift, then pull against the grain. My brother in his three-wheeled baby buggy. No rubber for a fourth wheel. And down the road, Johnny Haar, gassed in World War I, his face twisted into a smile. Drool down his chin, and his indecipherable sounds. Not quite a wail, not quite a moan, though my mother says *see how happy he is.*

Not a farm, but next door to a farm. Cornfields and pasture. Cows restless in their stanchions. *Mooooo.* They really do sound like the storybooks. Shifting of rumps. The call rises at the far end of the barn. Clank of metal as the cow swings her head, backfeet splayed. A ripple of flanks. *Moooo.* The answer, close now, louder, slobber of sound.

That was all before. When everything rose early. A rooster who haunted the rafters. When everything seemed large and familiar and unchanging. Then there was kindergarten and the world grew as small as a word. *C-o-w.* Which led to *h-o-w* and *v-o-w.* Which led in turn to the confusion of *low* and *mow* and *sow* and *tow.* And back to *now.* And later *bough* and *through* and *tough* and *thorough.* Small as a word, and unfamiliar.

———

Dawn. Three thousand miles away, I see it happen. Though I know you really can't see the mountains till noon. Gray in the morning, a filtered gray, all gauze and cautious cloudcover. Three thousand miles and three time zones, and I call up sunlight on snowcap.

Sundown, nightfall: the compound words of active disappearance. The Olympics, their dark serrated edges outlined in pink and gold. And then the solid dark. Eleven o'clock, which only days ago was midnight: the motion-sensored light in the backyard snaps on. We listen for something—a rattle of lids, a scratch of claws on the cement patio. What is out there in the night? Raccoon, the deer that stare back unafraid, apples falling behind the fence, the last long stretch to the solstice. This, I suspect, is nostalgia for the future.

Two hundred years ago, a day had its own slow cycle, full and round as the arc of the sun in the sky. No one conceived of today's digital dislocation. And then, with the Industrial Revolution, suddenly time belonged to someone else. The world shifted. Protestant time: doctrinal and unrepentant.

The long reach back to four years old—conjured memory— is not the same as nostalgia, which presumes a sense of time passing, the sense of self that says *mine, my time, my time,* over and over, a litany of hours. No, that was before time slipped through the fingers and made itself felt in its very dissipation. The sun rose, and fell. The men came with their tools, went back again to their quarters. My mother took down the clothes from the line with their hint of folded sunshine. My father came home from work and took up his hoe. Up one row, down another. What is a weed? What is a sun-ridden sky, and a world beyond it?

———

Time stops. Suspended there where to sit all afternoon on the front step is simply to sit all afternoon on the front step. Is to register the sound of duration in birdcall and breeze. Is to hear the blurred wings of a lawn mower, a dog punctuating the silence from two blocks away. One bark. A syncopated beat. Then two more. Then nothing. But a nothing full of the bark that did not follow, an ellipsis of sorts. And then, when you least expect it, when the throb of sunshine is all you can sense, another bark. Fainter, and less insistent.

Afternoons filled with time, as though it were solid and you could save it in your pocket. As though you could part it, like a curtain, and find yourself inside another room. Sometimes you did. You stepped right inside the pages and they held you up. Wherever you were, the book was all that contained you as you clambered over the locked garden wall. It knew you better than you knew yourself.

———

But some books were better than others. You knew enough to know that, even then. Some took the words that had floated free above you and anchored them to circumstance. The wall grew thick with vines. It became *your* secret.

Some were better than others, and you held the key—a huge black key that turned in the lock and allowed you entry. Indeterminate time, until your mother called you back for dinner, until bedtime came in its lockstep pace.

Those were the books that mattered. They were in you, the way waves, incessant, after a while cease to be sound. Even now, you can call up their timelessness. Not only *The Secret Garden* and *Little House on the Prairie,* but the chronicle of your maturation: *East of Eden, The Great Gatsby, Light in August*— west and east and south opening themselves to you long before you mounted the steps of the train, long before the summer you and your friend drove her sister's old Renault into Wyoming, where you had to wait two days for foreign tires to be shipped to Dubois from Cheyenne. West and east and south and suddenly there you were: in Dublin itself, its wet streets slick and shiny in the streetlights, seeming to leap from the pages of Joyce. Were you really there, or did the book take visible shape? You shivered a little in the rain and were glad of its physical reminder. You stepped back into time, into deadline and decision and detail.

———

Who were those men from the co camp? They came from Brooklyn, from Buffalo and Pittsburgh, brought together in our town through their shared refusal. Some were communists— innocent idealists of the sort that only America can produce. They were city men who knew nothing of farming. If they'd been from the west, we know they would have been pressed into fighting fires, building dams, clearing trails in the national parks. But in the east they were herded into a barracks and farmed out to do their farming. My father, Bob, was one of them.

Or not one of them, not quite. He was a physicist in a necessary job, so he was allowed to stay at home, allowed to go to work each day. He moved freely in and out of society. The best of both his worlds. By rights, they should have resented him.

I would have sensed it. I'd have felt their backs stiffen when they tossed me into the air. I'd have seen their eyes cloud over

whenever he came home, riding his bicycle the long seven miles, saving gasoline. They would have looked away, busy with their weeding. Instead, they looked up, called out the latest news on the radio. And they welcomed his hoe, adding to the rhythm of the long summer evening. Light languished. None of them knew— not even my father, the physicist—that Los Alamos was looming.

Here's what they thought: all wars are the same, and all are inhuman.

———

Some books are better than others. I say it into the void. I say it into an atmosphere filled with the explosive shards of theory. I say it in the face of a vocabulary that daunts even the dauntless, a jargon I cannot wrest from its abstract origins. Some books are better than others. They know more of the human heart, and more of its heartlessness. They are haunted by water. Haunted by what they cannot escape. Heart-rending. They are not cultural constructions. They are Johnny Haar—the pure, individual cry of the singular first person. His war was not the same—and it was inhuman. Time twists and conjoins like a Möbius strip, catches up from behind and places its shoes in its own parenthetical footprints.

We could name them: those brave voices that stand out from the crowd. We could name them, but our lists would not tally. Still, we would know what we mean: someone was there before me. Some one.

———

The body wakes in its old time zone. Shaken awake. All afternoon you sat on the step while the sun swept the sky. All afternoon you relived time. Dean Stockwell played Colin, you remember that. And now you see him on the screen, an aging man, a few years older than you are. Your mirror, if you needed one. Though anything will do: *Blue Suede Shoes* or *Wayward Wind;* paper dolls, the Brooklyn Dodgers, s&h Green Stamps. Green War Savings Stamps. My father's yard laid out in tidy rows: corn and carrots and onions and beets. The handwriting of a generation.

Yesterday the tall young woman who didn't know how to hold a pen. Caught it up in her fist, then twisted her wrist in order to print a couple of words. Where was the Palmer Method of her youth? That spiral of *O*'s uncoiling like a slinky. Something lost, something skittering away. So this is what it is to see time fly. To count the years, then the months, then the days. To feel the press of time even as the minutes quicken, even as everything moves in doublespeed, fastforward, a race to the finish.

Now there is only the page—and the way the day stops at the brink of it. You have no words for what the greatest writers do, and hardly any words for how they do it. But you know what it is to turn back the hands of the clock, stare out of your bedroom window into one long evening hour when the men are leaning on their hoes, talking softly about everything that will matter for the rest of your life. The heft of their words, the urgency of tone as they talk about missing their wives, about violence and war and the way they have had to look deep into their own capacities. And then your mother calls through the screen—coffee and cake—and they all come, laughing, into the house. Their sounds will weave through fifty years, faded and forgiving. You've forgotten their names: those men who would not fight. You wonder if they might have been mistaken. You know that you don't know what drove their moments of decision. All you can hear is the grate of metal on rock, the small *harumph* as a clump of dirt is pulled from the aggregate. The war ended and they went away. The mouse ran down. You went off to school.

In Half

IN THE UPPER-HALF version of the black-and-white, she almost looks as though she were trapped. This moment: my aunt Margaret braces for morning. In Kodachrome,

her bright red nightgown blazes, and the white gate streams with sunlight. Somewhere in Central America, she is a throb of color. The lower half is filigree. Her bare foot

steps through time as she insinuates herself into the street, enters its pulse of sound. In the larger world, war has ground to a halt in Europe, and somewhere her future

husband is gearing up to spend his time in occupied Japan. For this moment, though, she stares past me as though she could face down a fate that will find her soon enough.

And Endings?

STILL, THE STORIES POOL and eddy. My father went
under the surgeon's knife, and then he drowned. Or rather,
he simply didn't come up. Stayed there, alone with the
tumble of his thoughts, the thrum of his blood pulsing through
machines. Stayed there, keeping to himself the sum of his days,
the 100,000 heartbeats a day that added themselves each to
each, over and over, nearing three billion, ka-thump, ka-thump,
until we told them no, enough, and they wound down to nothing at all, silence heavy and thick in the room as my brother
closed the door behind him. And what is memory in the face of
that? Yet the pictures rise with such exactitude. The way he
laughed. His knobby knees. How much he loved a bowl of mus-
sels. The day the canoe tipped, tossing him into the water. The
night he hoisted me onto his shoulders and we walked through
the rising river as though there were nothing to fear.

2.

We have to accept the fact of uncertainty
and learn to live with it.

—ROBERTA WOHLSTETTER,
Pearl Harbor: Warning and Decision

Uncertainty

I.

It rides high in its saddle.

It shifts and plummets—swoops—drifts.

It is still: stiller than a held breath, stiller than water frozen in the birdbath, stiller than the color white.

It is wing-shaped, solemn, more silent than midnight.

It is framed in my mother's photo album, round and innocent and full of the future.

It spirals upward and falls back, exhausted, then begins to climb again.

It is tied like a fishing fly, filament of air, filament of light, yellow halo, black depth, circling a hook.

II.

"You will have to learn to live with uncertainty," he says. He is a doctor, a friend. What does uncertainty look like, I wonder, though I know what it feels like. It feels something like driving a long stretch of Highway 2 across the northeastern part of Montana. A place so bleak and desolate where sky meets land that there seems to be no definition. A place where the meaning of beauty is called into question—then reinforced. A change in the horizon, a ripple of ground that might be canyon or rock formation, a dilapidated shed poking its ribcage into the air, gas station, bar, or billboard, anything at all becomes, for me, something to be added to my list of aesthetic pleasures. And the land itself, like an abstract painting: green against blue, yellow against blue, tan against gray, dark against light. There is absolutely no road I'd rather drive than Route 2, straight into nowhere.

III.

Intricate, delicate. Intricate, delicate. The mantra rises, inspires. Exchange, exchange, substance and subject, matter and material, atmosphere and impression, feeling and conviction, oxygen and carbon dioxide, in and out and pull and push and change and change, world and body, thought and emotion, blend of word and blood and air. Inhale, exhale, breathe in, breathe out, inhale, exhale, over, over, over, over, over.

IV.

I have been happy in this house. This nondescript white rambler built in the seventies. I've been happy in its spaces, curled in the bed with a book and a cup of tea, or in my study, surrounded by photos and toys, goblets and marbles and an array of wooden boxes, looking out my window as the sky lightens in the east where I came from but do not miss. I've been happy looking out—at the deer who use our backyard as their trail, at the way the wind flays the branches on the hill but does not spill down into our yard so that we are tucked away by the fire, untouched. I was not happy in my other three houses: the fake stucco Tudor, or the authentic old colonial, or the genuine large Victorian. I played at being happy in each of them, but they held my play-acting up to me more often than not. Their corners and closets could not contain my longings. I am glad to have found this modest house where I can spread out my colors in peace.

V.

What is a lung? A tissue of fabric that fills us with air, lifts us into the day. I know its shape. With extreme precision, with pinpoints of pain, it draws itself on my back—as though, if I could twist my arms backwards, they could trace the outline, wing-shaped. And then the body itself would fly off on its own small shuttle of air. In and out, in and out, breath fills you with light. Below that, the heaviness, the dark interiors. But the lung—it reaches up, and out, as though it knew more than the body's horizons.

VI.

In my dream, I can move easily. I get out of the car and walk around to the other side, where I pick up two packages to take inside the house. I do this over and over, all night long. It feels so natural, lugging the packages, walking around the car, again and again. This is something I cannot do now in daylight. So at night I long for the ordinary. That, or else it's the drug that turns my dreams on its spit, round and round, basting memory into those moments when I wake to the dream that spins itself out in what seems like real time. I slip back into sleep, and there I am, once more, lifting and lugging myself into the house.

VII.

What do I love of this world? I mean, besides the people who populate my life, my dream of the people I love. I surround myself with objects, and I love them, in part, for what they say about what I want to love. But suppose I were asked to list ten things. Only ten. What would I want to pack in my bag and take with me? The final two paragraphs of Norman Maclean's *A River Runs Through It;* Robert Frost's "The Oven Bird"; one red Fiestaware pitcher, with its radioactive isotope; Benjamin Britten's way with Wilfred Owen's poems, the music so carefully orchestrated you almost miss it, almost forget that it's there; one painting by William—I'll take the one where the water glazes over, rainslick on the canvas; one reel on the fiddle by Matthew, fast, and then faster; odd little cedar-bark basket made by June Ward of Neah Bay, given to me by Stan, its orange-tipped canoe a flash on gray water; a turquoise necklace I once owned, and lost, though my fingers can still feel its heft; and, oh the cards and drawings—Benjamin, Simon, Ian—creatures of their infinite minds; maybe those small blue irises in the planter on the deck or the scent of garlic lingering on my fingers, but those are transient, more air than stone, more mood than bone, and should they count? There are other things, there must be, but wouldn't these few be sufficient? And why worry? These are the shapes of certainty that I will have to learn to give up.

VIII.

The sights of my morning:

out of the fog, a bird glides, wings spread, up and into the tree outside my window;

rain, plink, plink, landing on the bamboo leaves, trickle, flicker, each leaf unloads its burden—dip, release, shiver;

like breath on a winter morning, smoke from the neighbor's chimney rises into the fog and soon the question: how can we tell one thing from another;

blue glass goblet, red glass bird, pink swirl of flower in the paperweight, window lit with what it lights;

gray sky, flat and sulky, silken skein of weather, whether it will turn blue later, later will not be soon enough.

IX.

Lost enough weight that I can justify new underwear. Now my mother's nightmare might not come true: white cotton, stretched sloppy at the waistband and a bit stained, a couple of holes, a tear in the fabric, defining me in the emergency room. Now I might arrive, newly sized, still white cotton, but white as in still new, buttressing my idea of myself. I've never been lace. Not even in dreams. Never been silk, or black, or silvery lilac. Clouds of steam. Clouds of wishful, papery words. My mother drifts away, like snow.

X

Who knew air could feel so heavy? Could weigh you down? You measure it, pushing, pushing it back at the world. Make it go out, you think, make it make its impression.

Who knew words could fly in the face of their origins? Could confuse and obfuscate merely by using their science against you? I read and I read and still I cannot fathom what "oxidation" means that I should so want to resist it. I read and I read and fact becomes my enemy. Fact: I have always loved fact. Fact: I want to embrace fact. Fact: I want my own sense of reality here, and this is not learning to live with uncertainty, though it may be one step along the way.

Step. That is what I cannot do. Step on out into the world. Not without the heaviness—tons of it—that settles into the knees and won't let go. It's the weight of air, the extreme heaviness of its reduced volumes, coiling its bulk at my knees.

XI.

You are never the patient. Even when you empathize with the patient, you are imagining what is happening to the patient, and that is not what is happening to you. You think about how you would like to handle the situation—*if* you were the patient. But you are not the patient, and you can't know how you would respond. Until one day you are the patient, and then you think about whether you are being the one you imagined, or someone wholly else, someone who can't quite believe this is happening at all.

XII.

All night, the body rumbling through the dark, the locomotives of my childhood, *chuffa chuffa chuffa chuffa,* up and out of the valley, away, away, streaking past the sleeping village, its lone light prying open the darkness. Up and away, the dream of the child rising, too, following the tracks into what might never be known. *Chuffa, chuffa, chuffa, chuffa,* out into the places found in her books: Scotland, Brazil, moors, and a deep blue sea. Out into places that settle, like salt, into the blood. Recall them now, as the body hustles its air in and out, raise them up in memory: stone cottage huddled into the hillside, lone piper pumping air into air until the whole spit shivers under its plaintive wail; white walls shimmering under relentless sun, the urubus: strange, distant vultures, riding the thermals as though they were toying with air.

XIII.

There are hard, tough questions. And I ask them of myself, of others. Hard, tough decisions I want to be able to make. Hard, tough places I will need to return to, need to hold on to as the soft tissues harden, and the soft air comes and goes.

XIV.

Here is the CT scan. I carry my lungs on a silver disk, carry the stiff, white spots that line my lungs in such exquisite symmetry. She will "read" my lungs, will show me the perfect black hole where the air goes in, the places it somehow cannot move through. She will tell me I must learn to live with uncertainty, even as we decide on the certain pills I will take, the certain plans I must make, the certain directions of this uncertain terrain I have entered.

XV.

Over the phone, people comment on how well I sound. I do sound well, especially when I laugh, and I look well, too. Well, except when I walk, and you can see how unsteady I am. Well, except for the chipmunk cheeks that let slip my telltale medicine.

XVI.

Should I order those new clothes I like from the catalog?

Should I keep on designing and redesigning a new kitchen—one where I will actually make meals, mess up, clean up, make meals again?

Should I accept that invitation for next fall? Should I? Can I? Will I?

All the questions that rise like yeast in future tense seem fraught with contingency. But a question mark implies uncertainty, and I use the question mark all the time. Did I already know how to live with uncertainty? Or has it shed new light on my now-cautious days?

XVII.

Candled egg. Lit from within. Lung-shaped, lit from within. My candled future, what it used to be, what it is becoming.

XVIII.

Who are you to make something beautiful of your own condition? To romanticize what is, essentially, something more important than your writing? Who are you to reduce yourself in that way? Or elevate yourself in that way? To make yourself the center of your own attention? How dare you rob your husband of wife, your children of mother, your grandchildren of someone they still need to know? How dare you sit underneath this window and look out at a flat white sky and imagine yourself gone on into its limitlessness?

Limit yourself, then. Limit yourself to the books that you love, the words you have written—the ones you still own. Limit yourself to the letters that came to you, filed in your left-hand drawer. To the gifts you've been given—the boxes and baskets and stones from the beach, and the faded, ethereal flowers. Limit yourself to the tangible. Touch the wrinkle of skin on your arm where the lost weight has turned you into your grandmother.

Touch your face, as though it were unfamiliar. Learn what it is that you are, now that you've made yourself up.

XIX.

Today nineteen is my favorite Roman numeral: *x-i-x*, its symmetry somehow perfected, two unknowns flanking the *I*.

XX.

My specialist clearly never learned cursive. She takes four minutes to print out my instructions. She writes notes in one-word increments, slantwise. One word. Cursory. Not enough to remind her that this is complicated, and exacting. I want to tell her my "affairs" are in order, my drawers are all clean, my books are in alphabetical order on my shelves. I want to tell her she is too young for me. She takes forever to laboriously sign her name on the prescription—the only cursive in sight.

XXI.

If, as I don't believe, we are sometimes punished in this life, then I am being punished for being judgmental. I will admit to judgment, sharp and sometimes not too kind. Can't help it though. I judge. I find people guilty. I hope that I also find myself guilty—but I know that I don't all that often. I don't forgive lying, or laziness, or what I think of as willed lack of knowledge. I don't forgive inadequacy, not when it seems deliberate, rationalized, or somehow excused. What is the excuse for doing a bad job of something—especially in thinking about how you want your own life to be lived?

XXII.

The rain on the needles of the lodgepole pine across the street shines in the sun so that the whole tree is backlit, a tippling swirl of light that shakes itself loose and drops toward the ground. It might be metaphor for something, but for the life of

me I can't think of what. It's simply morning rain on a suddenly windswept day, the sun showing its face, and my window
just happening to face its brief appearance. From this angle, I
do not see the road, the houses, the telephone wires. I see only
a perimeter of hectic branches, briefly glittering. And inside,
ringing the window: my grandfather, my father, my mother, my
aunt Margaret, my brother, my husband, my sons, my daugh-
ters-in-law, my grandsons, even myself as a curious girl, staring back at me.

XXIII.

I have been given prayers, floating in cyberspace. Prayers and
prayer flags and healing circles and a homeopath and support
groups and herbs too numerous to mention. My name has been
shouted out at someone's Rock Shabbat. *Listen,* I want to
shout. I want respect for my own beliefs: science, hard thought,
cold fact.

XXIV.

Three months, January to April, and now it looks as though
these lungs will turn me back to the breathing. One uncertainty seems less uncertain. Out my window, I notice evening's
slow encroachment. The sky is dimming, perceptibly, and I
know that behind me, at the back of the house, the sun will
soon sink below the hill, maybe in a blaze of red and pink, more
likely simply painting the clouds with an opaque silver under-
lining. Down at the strait, the sunset will be strident on the
water and the waves will catch its color as they roll in. But what
I am seeing, now, here, this moment, is the sky going darker
and, on the tips of the trees, a shivering glance of light before
it disappears. In the yard across from me, three deer try to
reach through mesh to nibble the sapling willow. Later they
will wander through our yard on the way to our neighbor's
apple trees. They will bound up the hillside, fluid and unafraid.

The clouds will turn pewter, dark as an impending storm, and the trees will begin their frenzy in a gust that is portrayed on our TV as a furious mix of arrows, as though wind itself were military. If I wait patiently at my window, I will see at least one crow—the color of night—sweep across my horizon. I will wish he would make his presence known, but he will be silent and swift, and capricious.

3.

What had *happened would seem to loom*
with the mystery of what will *happen*

—STUART DYBEK

Absolute Grey

IN THE GRAYSCALE PALETTE, it's gray, with an *a*. Hardworking half-and-half of the photograph. But this grey is different—weighted with the past, elegant and restrained. Prepositional. It carries with it mystery, the question mark, uncertainty's elusive *why*. Degree of fog. Tincture of remorse. It rubs itself with ash. Becomes the fur of the cat next door, slinking off into twilight in absolute silence, absolutely certain of its way.

Young Woman on Fence

I STARE AT THE TIRE because to look at her, perched on the fence, feet on the top of the tire, hands open in a suggestive shrug, is to ask questions I can't answer. To look at her there, in her man's white shirt, sport coat, and tie, is to transport yourself to every dream you ever had when you were growing up. *Did you know your daughter was playing baseball without her shirt, just like the boys?* To look at her face with its sunken eyes, hidden behind glasses, framed by ambiguous hair, cut short—a bob, I think they would have called it—is to look at the self you did not dream of.

Cut the photo in half horizontally and you, too, sit on the white rail fence. It moves from left to right, like a line of type, a sentence stretched to its fullest. Cut it in half vertically and you leave one side blank, bereft of any interest. The right side fills with her, darkens and delineates. Now she is going nowhere. She is merely sitting there, staring at the lens. Her mouth does not lift in recognition. She stares into history, writing herself: young woman on fence.

The tire is an *O*, a zero, an egg. The day revolves around it. Oh, we exclaim, as it cuts across the great equal sign of the rails. Oh, we say, she is both man and woman, balanced at the cusp of what she might be. *Did you know that your daughter was playing baseball?* Oh, we say, and Oh, as the mystery deepens, the cervix effaces, letting in light.

It is the thirties. Or late twenties. Who could tell? The album gives no names, no places, no clues. My mother must have known her—why else would she be glued so tightly to the page? My mother could have given me her name, a hazy sense of the day. Of what lay behind that enigmatic mouth. But I cannot ask my mother because she is gone. Somewhere in Michigan, I guess, because most of my mother's young life was played out there. Michigan, 1929, I say, end of a decade that led to the moment she lifted that tie from her brother's closet, shoved her arms neatly into his sleeves.

Paris. It's possible. She could have found a place in Paris. If she had enough personality, she would be the talk of the town. Give herself a new name. Paule. She would give up Polly, silly name for someone growing up on a farm, more like the cows. 'M'on Boss, 'm'on Bess, 'm'on Moll, 'm'on Sal. So many evenings, calling them in to the barn. 'M'on Daisy, you little pill. The light going down on the pasture, like spilled milk, the horizon white for an instant, then dusk. If she had the personality, she could leave that behind. The cafés in late afternoon, glasses spread across the tables like so many empty suns, talk of where to go to eat, talk of where to go afterwards, where to meet—the studio, or the salon. Light clustered there at the foot of the street, shutters ringing with light, the rooftops a plight of pigeons. Wings lifting into evening air, dark against light, a rush of feathered memory. 'M'on Poll.

Dirt road, wildflowers, maybe weeds, maybe clover. It's very early spring—the trees are barely in leaf. Little furls of bud, if you could see them, but you can't. She can't see them. They are behind her, calling *this is your home*. But she has turned her back on them. She is staring at someone, but it takes you a while to remember that. Her stare seems set on someplace deep into the future. She looks beyond the camera that would hold her there on the fence. So you forget there are two people in this photograph, and that she has a willing accomplice. Male or female? Is it the brother who only this morning jokingly handed her his tie so they would set off like boys, wind in their hair? Is it her sister, her friend, someone in need of an escort? Her skirt brushes across her knee as she kneels, lifts the camera, finds the perfect angle. Or another young woman—*Did you know that your daughter?*—dressed in her own father's shirt, the two of them larking about the tangled miles of rural Michigan, waiting out summer for when they will leave for New York, adventure at their heels?

It's 1929. Or 1935. If I could know, then I would know what lies ahead for each of them. Maybe it's already too late, and she cannot leave for a Paris that soon will hear the sounds of bootsteps in its streets. The fence falling into disrepair. A father with his head in his hands, a mother's illness. Maybe a younger brother, the knife of war already poised over his unsuspecting head. So much held in balance. The tire will be mended (small patch of black rubber) and she will turn back to her closet filled with dresses and shoes. She will turn back to a blue plaid apron and a Sunday hat. She will turn back into Polly, who left the farm for Detroit.

Did you know that? I learned how to be a boy from my books. I could have watched my brother, or my friends, but that would have made it bearable. 'M'on Boss, 'm'on Babe, 'm'on Boss. Strike 'im out. 'M'on Boss. Too easily seen through. Translucent. First, I was Colin, but who wanted to be sickly? So I chose Dicken, who could roam the moors and bring back what he found. Gorse blossom, yellow in daylight. Thorned at night. And after that I chose my own names, strange combinations of Robert of Bruce, Duncan, names that carried with them the lochs at daybreak. A solitude of names, ringing inside me. I learned how to be a boy from roaming the moors, each day farther than the day before. To be a boy was to be free from the eyes that told me who I should be.

Five years, and my mother will almost imagine me into being. I'll come with the war. My mother will paste the photo—*Did you?*—into the album, laughing a little at their escapades, that is, if it was also her escapade. Let's give it to her. Who is left to deny it? In sixty years, I'll open the album and this young woman will be sitting there still, shrugging off the flat white sky. Now I look at her hands, so expressive as they open themselves to the world. I see what I failed to see before. This is the end of the story; she's the one who has had to change this tire. She's splaying her fingers to show us—you and me—that they're covered in deep, dark Michigan mud.

Girls in White Dresses

WATCH MY MOTHER blossom. She unfurls in slow motion—six to sixteen to twenty-six. Nothing in this sequence tells me her story. Nothing looks like a girl growing up poor on a farm. And yet I know they had no money. Egg money must have paid for the photographer, paid for the props to make her a princess. Here's what I know: she hated that photo, the one in which she's a beauty. Hated the V of the neck. What could have made her so proper? Surely it wasn't her mother, whose life was all work and no play but who was known for her good sense of humor. Whatever it was, I am sorry. Her dresses spell snowdrop and trillium. Orchid. Water lily.

"Some of Lillian's Friends from North Adams—Note Car"

MUSES OF MICHIGAN—Calliope, Urania, Euterpe, Thalia, Melpomene, Erato, Terpsichore, and Polyhymnia—looking quite contemporary under that 1920s sky. They giggle their way into our lives, shedding their skirts for designer jeans, their stockings for tattoos. Nine of them pose, dressing their parts, poised on running board and rumble seat—even the roof. Wait! There—only her stockings and shoes to show us she's present—is Clio, muse of history. Who will drive them all down the long dirt road?

"Note car," she says, but to whom is she speaking? When is she writing? Certainly not then—it's in ballpoint ink. And why, when we clearly can't help but note it? Don't all those old cars look alike? It takes some research to be definitive: a Ford Model T Roadster, probably 1917 or '18, just after the war, everything expanding, optimism reaching its peak. By the time they climb on in their new short hair, the car must be at least five years old, already a bit outmoded, already headed toward the Depression none of them can see around the bend. "Note car," she says, as she takes one last look before she pastes them into her past. Halfway between then and now, she positions herself in third person, naming herself as though she were there among them. Note car, as they hurl themselves into this moment while I watch her watching the wind in their hair.

Parentheses

"LILLIAN & JACK (on the farm)"—that's what it says. This must be while she was still in college or maybe high school, before she left for good. She looks so content in her simple plaid skirt on the solid front porch. I'd say it was spring—she's in shirtsleeves, there are clothes on the line, and the tree is budding with leaf. At the right, there's a hint of a pillar. She positions herself (or she's been positioned) where dark and light meet. I like her here on the farm, where she's so plain and no-nonsense. I like the way she seems completely at home.

This photograph must be elegy, since outside the frame we sense a young woman making her way away from the furrows and fencerows. The farm will recede to a pinpoint—a parenthetical place she will explain to others, while her heart lifts its complex (it must be) of feelings as she pastes herself here in its two-by-three inches of loss.

Recess

Tues. 10:00 a.m. (Recess)
Lillian dear,
   Am I dreaming, or am I awake? I pinch myself every once in awhile to see if I am. I am so thrilled I don't know whether I am teaching geography or arithmetic. I am eating and sleeping Europe. Just think, Lillian, all those places we have always dreamed of, we will see, and that wonderful voyage across (if we are not seasick!). A doctor told me not to eat any meat or fats of any kind for a couple of weeks before sailing. Sailing!! Doesn't the word conjure up visions of delight. If I could just be sure I won't be feeding the fishes. I must go and ring the bell.

Now my youngsters are studying and I have a minute to spare. I have to keep one eye on the paper and one on them. I will send you a money order tomorrow so you can order me one (a steamer trunk). I know I will have one grand scramble packing all the things I want to take into it. Are you taking a weekend bag besides that? You know, it spoke about that in the booklet. It seems to me that it would be almost necessary.
   I went home last weekend and didn't get your first letter until I came back Sunday night. You can imagine how elated I was. My poor roommate hears Europe continually and plans for clothes and all that. It rather surprised me that we would need a formal. I may get one ready made and have Grandma make one. Now I am going to Europe

probably just once in a lifetime and I am not going to miss a trick if I can help it. I am going to look like an animated crane in a formal but I don't care. I hope they have softly shaded lights so that my freckles won't show up too much. I haven't the slightest idea what I will get yet. Oh, it is going to be such fun getting clothes. That is the best part of it. I wish that we might go shopping together, but of course that is impossible. It would be such fun to get them in Detroit. I envy you your opportunity. I suppose you will appear all "dogged out." This is the one spree of my lifetime and even if I am the rest of my life paying back the debt, I am going to make a desperate attempt to have some good-looking clothes. I am going home this week-end, I think.

Love, Joan

When you get any more information be sure and send it along. Of course we share the same stateroom, don't we?

Three Cheers!

Bon Voyage!

Au Revoir!

and any other suitable expressions you can think of.

Love, Joan

Trueheart

THE JOURNAL IS DARK LEATHER, embossed in gold with "A Record of My Tour Abroad." Which is just what my mother did—record. June, 1930: Europe caught between two wars, my mother's world expanding. The twenties a wisp of memory as the country rushed pell-mell toward its future.

I open the book to see what was in store for her: flags of all nations, a list of currencies and exchanges, practical tips on everything from luggage to taxis to hotel protocol. "Be sure that your shoes are comfortable, and on shipboard, rubber soles and heels are desirable." And after that, the diary begins.

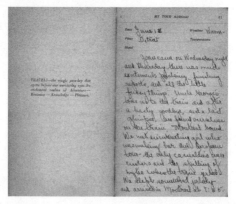

I turn the pages to meet the young woman I've seen before— the one whose hair is hidden under a dark cloche, standing at the rail of a ship, arms linked with another woman whose hair flies away in the wind. My mother's dress is dark, with tiny white buttons running down its length, a white collar and—yes—white cuffs. White stockings, too, like the ones worn by her friend whose scarf is thrown carelessly around her neck and whose shoes, with their low heels and delicate strap, give her the shapely look of someone ready for something. My mother's shoes are the giveaway. Sturdy, flat-heeled shoes that lace. Practical. Good for walking. Good for practically everything—except letting your hair fly out.

Standing at the brink of something large, my mother looks down, and away from the lens. What will she learn about herself as she embarks on this journey? I read to find out:

JUNE 14
There was a movie on board—but we couldn't see—too many spectators. We danced to a rather blarey electric victrola.

The stewards are the best looking and most interesting people we have met yet. They wear dark blue uniforms with brass buttons and white caps with blue bands and gold lettering. The lounge steward is adorable—he helps to serve tea in the afternoon and he has a charming smile. The dining room steward is nice too—and the captain is dignified, stalwart and commanding looking. We learned how to put on life-savers today.

The photograph was taken early in the trip (the word "leaving" is written lightly in the upper left-hand corner) on board the *Letitia,* maybe even as it sailed up the St. Lawrence, past Quebec ("lights and lights and blue water and steamers") and on out into the Atlantic. Maybe before the month (and what a month!)—Glasgow, Edinburgh, Birmingham, Shakespeare country, London, The Hague, Amsterdam, Brussels, Cologne,

Wiesbaden, Heidelberg, Interlaken, Lucerne, Munich, Oberammergau, Innsbruck, Venice, Florence, Rome, Genoa, Nice, Avignon, Paris—had worked its magic.

So who is the young woman who looks almost ready to open herself to experience? She has grown up an only child on a farm near North Adams, Michigan—her childhood pinched by poverty. She has worked her way through high school, leaving the farm to "live-in" with a family in town where she takes care of their four children after school. She has worked her way through college as a waitress, spending the long summers working at a resort just south of the Mackinaw Strait. She has found her first job teaching school. And now she is ready:

JUNE 24

Our tour proper began today. We left the hotel early, and it was raining. We took the train 1st to Loch Lomond—the trains have 1st, 2nd, and 3rd class and are divided off into tiny rooms with 2 long seats facing each other. They hold about 10 people, that is, each compartment does. We rode 3rd class and the coaches weren't bad at all. Then we took a lake steamer and went across Loch Lomond. It was really beautiful—altho' the rain spoiled full appreciation and we were somewhat disappointed. The mists and fogs hung heavily over the tops of the mountains. Then we alighted and what do you suppose conveyed us next? Open carriages drawn by 4 horses (called tally-hoos). They carried about 20 people, each. It was raining when we started and continued to rain all day.

To whom is she writing this journal? Her question presupposes someone who will share her surprise. As the month goes on, the writing does not deepen into observation, yet it becomes more intensely private, less a record and more a shorthand. A spur. In the end, she seems to be writing for the self she will have become after a dozen years: wife, mother, early-middle-aged woman with memories to resurrect:

We went to see the Pope's Palace in Avignon and an old bridge. After dinner, Anne, Eliz. & I went to a French show—had fun watching the people—but I went to sleep & finally we left. Leanna & Laura & 2 other girls met a fellow from Yale who was driving his mother thru Europe & they all rode everywhere & never got in until 7 this morning. I went to sleep about 12, I guess, and this morning Joan & I discussed weighty subjt.—& we've decided that 'love rules everything so we want to be ruled by it, too.'

There's a terrible innocence here, an innocence I don't remember ever feeling. I'd like to warn this young woman about life. I'd like to warn her before late July, when she will ascend the gangplank of the *Tuscania* and find her stateroom (112F). I'd like to have a talk with her before she returns home. Before she meets a man called Trueheart with his fascinating tales of his roommate Jo Jo, a millionaire's son who every so often feels the need to rebel.

What does a proper young schoolteacher do when she meets the likes of Trueheart? She breaks her heart, that's what. But not before she learns more than she bargains for. This young lady, who meticulously records the churches and bridges of Europe, the gloves and bags and shoes and cuff links of her shopping sprees, the names of all the other young women and how they are "smart dressers" or "sweet girls"—this young lady who goes to bed before everyone else—what does she do when life offers something up to the imagination? When T. H. walks into her life? Or, rather, into the shipboard life, which is never *the* life, but some brief respite from it.

My mother does not recognize this as respite. This feels like the real thing. The long lists of castles and operettas and mountains are merely the backdrop in which this ship has a context. Michigan is tiny in her lens. The ocean stretches to the horizon day after day—and T. H. comes to dominate the diary. Why does he choose her, my fairly plain mother? Even she has recognized the vivacity of the others—the blond hair of Ayleen from Louisiana, the way Leanna says "Oh"—drawled in a note of supreme thrilldom—"honey." These are the ones who might understand what he was all about. But that's just why he chooses her—because she *is* so innocent. He chooses to spend this suspended time with someone who does not know she is in a state of suspension.

Oh, I know, I'm reading between the lines. I'm bringing to her diary my own odd predilections. In the face of very little evidence, I give her the story she should have had.

She's restless, and receptive, this lively young woman who can trounce Trueheart at deck tennis, whose laugh seems so light, as though it were a bluebird's feather. And her story intrigues him. At last he has something to offer. He can leave this innocent dark-haired girl with a taste for romance. He will initiate her in the art of living. Of wanting something from her life. So he asks her to dance. He asks her to play shuffleboard. He is her partner for bridge, and deck tennis, and hearts. He asks her to dance once more, to the tinny tunes that seem to find a fullness all their own in the mild salt air. The two of them walk the moonlit decks. They break into song. Everything such a night was meant to be, this one is. She thinks of her mother on the farm, of her old dog Jack, of the sorrel mare. At dinner the next evening—the second seating—she thinks back to when she worked as a waitress, how her feet always ached. But her feet do not ache on this ship, and besides, she's bought new shoes just for this occasion.

My mother cannot believe her good fortune. She cannot believe that she has been singled out by someone so dashing to learn the rules of love. I want to warn her. After all, I have the ending at my disposal. At the back of her journal, she has collected names and addresses, she lists the "pet expressions" of her friends, she writes down directions for how to perform a variety of card tricks, and she records the hierarchy for poker, beginning with royal flush and descending to one pair. The back of her journal tells it all: under T, there is no address for Trueheart. He does not plan to extend this romance. He already knows what she has yet to learn—that once they step off the boat, their old lives will claim them again.

So, in my mind, my mother dreams. She wonders how she will take him to the farm, and what he will make of her parents. She even wonders how she will introduce him to the principal of the school where she works and what she will say. My mother is carried away, and I envy her the fact that she cannot look, yet, as I do now, at the back of her book, cannot realize where it is heading. Because she's going there quickly—eight pages left before she will document her sighting of the Statue of Liberty:

AUG. 3
And then all of a sudden—was the old Goddess herself standing calmly in the breeze. I could have wept. Despite my despise of sentimentality—I was awfully near it then as Glenna & I fondly clasped hands and gazed at her unruffled countenance.

Thirteen pages to go before this account will end on the train back to Michigan:

*Joan & I parted at Jackson—
but we're going
to go again maybe
for it was all
just too good
to be true.*

Hindsight offers me insight. They did not go again. My mother's life, as most lives do, fell into its series of choices, leading inevitably to her marriage, and then eventually to me. I am the beneficiary. I inherited all: her stories, her scrapbook, her photo album. This small leather book, a bit worse for wear.

Here's what I know: she spoke often of the friends she made on her trip. She wrote to them at Christmas and received cards in return, received letters recounting the ways their lives had branched away from each other. The time she spent that summer stayed alive in her. She never once mentioned the name of Trueheart, not even in passing. I know. I would have remembered. I would have heard the slight change in her timbre, the way her voice thickened before she said his name. If love ruled the world, then lack of it was all-powerful. My father came in Trueheart's wake.

———

A journal, dark leather, embossed in gold: I open the pages in order to meet the young person I never knew. I am tempted to say there are vestiges there of the woman who was my mother, but that would be putting the cart before the horse. This is the opposite of vestige—the cloth from which the remnants will come. And so I half recognize this woman who calls herself a "girl." I recognize her girlishness. I recognize its opposite. And, oh god, I recognize her shoes.

I have the impulse to give her more than she seems to have given herself. That's why I spin the story of Trueheart. He'd have to be a fiction, wouldn't he, with a name like that? Though he's there all right, there in the final flurry of the diary, monopolizing its pages. But there was no shipboard romance. No dreams of the future. Or, if there were, I will never know it for certain. He's there, sentence after sentence, reduced to T. H. to make him more palatable, more seemingly offhand and insignificant. He's there—playing bridge *("I got peeved at T. H. because he took back a card fairly played"),* he's there on deck (with Glenna, Eliz. & Willis and my mother) singing—no, "pouring forth" song after song: "Girl of my Dreams," "Memories," "Sweetheart of Sigma Chi," and "Moonlight and Roses." He's there, arguing about *"Prohibition, economics, immigration and everything" (Glenna and I are in favor of Prohibition)";* he's there when the "war-horse (Icile B.)" comes along and "gurgles" about T. H.'s photograph and wants one for her memory book *("Tee hee, etc. until I nearly yelled").* He's even there at the very end, just before customs and the train ride back to Detroit. In an entry that might easily be a scene in a thirties comedy, Trueheart is at the center:

AUG. 3
We dashed about excitedly—& then a call came for T. H. to go to the Purser's office. They tried to accuse him of being a Russian attempting to enter the U.S. He had his passport, of course, which convinced them. He thinks someone sent word just out of spite or else for a joke—for they had a radiogram or something to that effect.

Yes, he's there, but I've supplied the dreaming. I've given my mother the inner life she didn't give herself. There were dances—she mentions them—but did he dance with her? We will never know, yet I *want* to know. I want to make some connection with this woman before I am forced to step into her life, so I'm to be forgiven for reading between the lines. Look at her response to Icile B. It's clear—isn't it?—that my mother was smitten. That even though she puts on a brave front, she is desperately hoping for something more. That the next step will be her broken heart. That I will be the product of the rebound.

And who knows? I may be more right than you think. After all, I knew the woman she became. I was the recipient of Trueheart's legacy, which took two forms: an incurably romantic inclination for adventure and, simultaneously, an austere, judgmental desire to clamp down on pleasure.

Europe with another war simmering, unrecognized as the gondola tips and all of Venice seems to tilt. Maybe that story, too, is buried somewhere beneath my mother's almost-purple prose. For example, what do I make of the way she seems to repeat, almost verbatim, what the guides have told her?

JUNE 25
Edinburgh Castle—one high rock or hill towering like a mt.
in the midst of the city. This castle dates back even to about
900 B.C. where there was a fortress there. Situated as it is, it is
by nature a strong forthold, and approach is difficult. The
entire structure is of stone, of course, built right into the rock.
We saw the one-time moat and drawbridge and portcullis, the
artillery, the armoury or old banqueting room, the well they
kept covered when the place was taken.

But what did she think, or feel? She does not say. If she is writing for herself, will she be able—just with a word—to call it up again intact? Will the word "castle" bring back the dank wind at her back and the sense that history is about to come alive? Will the word "Edinburgh" call up the bright colors of the gardens, and somber stately buildings that fade into the sooty dusk? Will the red plaid blanket she bought in a shop be enough to overwhelm her with what she doesn't know? But that is myself I am describing, because my mother's book does not reveal someone who is overwhelmed. Not at all. It reveals someone to whom life is happening. She is going along. She does not seem burdened with my infernal urge toward retrospection.

Where is my mother in this writing? I sense nothing but a cipher. What did she *see*—beyond what she *saw*? There is little to give her away, not even in the next sentence—"We saw the dogs' graveyard, and the Memorial to the World War Soldiers"—with its marvelous collective innocence. Nine years later, and that sentence would be obsolete.

Only occasionally does she flirt with description, flirt with an audience of more than one:

JULY 5
We had too thrilling a trip today—riding by motor thru the
Alps. I felt like Hairbreadth Harry flirting with death. We

wound in and out and up & down. Elizabeth & I broke the monotony by having one of our numerous arguments. We saw the huge glacier—The Blue Grotto—and went thru it part way by a tunnel—and our faces looked ghastly in that icy blue light. We were quite warm when we got to Lucerne—but we all "dogged up" for dinner anyway.

I want to be sympathetic. I want to like her more than I do. And she is not unlikable—this increasingly unfamiliar woman who seems so full of life. But she is *so* innocent—innocent in a way that, if I am honest, bores me. Or bores my sixty-some-year-old self, the one who looks back on my own youth and cannot recognize myself in her. The one who knows what is going to happen, knows that my mother will not change enough to suit me. But a flip of the page and I find myself intrigued:

We went shopping after dinner and some of us broke up into 2 parties. Finally Ruth, Joan, & I came back to the hotel and danced with 3 unknowns.

At this point she gets coy. Whatever happened, we can only guess, because my mother has veiled it in a private code, visual mnemonics meant only for her. The page leaps from the book with a life all its own. At last, the stuff of literature: narrative, intrigue, consequence—and a sense of something consciously withheld. But why?

Clearly, she wanted to remember, but this was accessible only to herself. She hoarded the moment for the future—and handed the mystery down to me.

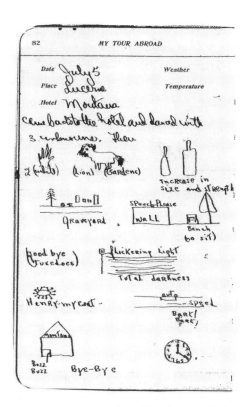

All of this took place before Trueheart. Before the long, oceanbound time of transition.

No, that's not quite right. That was only true when I was giving my mother a story—a final shipboard fling before she went back to the classroom. Now I have to be more vigilant. I have to stick to what I know. I go back to the book to read the actual lines and here it is—the first mention of Trueheart, hardly worth noting:

JULY 7
In the afternoon on the train we played bridge—Laura & I against Leanna & Trueheart. We didn't have such good luck, but finally Willis came along and he & I had good luck. We played "follow the leader" thru all the coaches—and had a

pillow battle, chinned ourselves, sang, and "made whoopee."
Then Anne & I put on our little "vaudeville stunt." She does
it much better than I, however. When we came to
Oberammergau we were much surprised. The people are so
different.

Go on, I urge her, let us see you strut your stuff. Whatever
you mean by "making whoopee"—and it's not what we mean by
that phrase today—go on and do it. I forget Trueheart for a
moment in my desire to have her be someone completely exotic.
But no, she will not let me into her thoughts. She goes back to
the job at hand.

So I can't help wondering, where has T. H. been all this while,
as my mother describes the red coats and tall hats of the British
guards, the windmills of Holland and the glacier's blue haze?
Why does he suddenly emerge on the train from Munich in the
middle of a game of bridge, less interesting than the "vaudeville
stunt" that so intrigues me?

JULY 12
We discussed disclosed faults & virtues and the biggest subjects
of all—"It" and "Love." I learned some interesting things
about myself. I haven't an abundance of "it," so Willis says—
and Anne told me something too nice to be true. The day
wouldn't be complete without a fight with Trueheart—and so
Bob Philips & Betty, Eliz., Anne, T. H. & I battled over the
cookies. It was night when we reached Venice—and sure
enough there were gondolas there to meet us. They took us thru
dark canals and to our hotel. Our room & its mosquito netting
canopies around the beds, the dark canals & everything thor-
oughly frightened Joan & I.

It isn't until July 21, on the train to Paris, that he becomes
more than passing reference. The written focus of her attention:

We got into a heated discussion over religion, the negro, Indians, and war. Everyone had an opinion but Trueheart had sound arguments. More & more he impresses one as the Southern gentleman—polite—lovely manners—intelligent—quiet—good taste—a thoroughbred. He must come from wealthy parents for they keep servants.

Ah, Trueheart, you are not the cad I made you out to be. Or not quite. Though what am I to do with the enigmatic sentences that come later, on the ship home? The places where she says, "*We played some bridge and later, Joan & I went to bed. I wonder why? The rest is better left unsaid.*" Or, the next day, "*This might better be left blank—(a bad memory).*" Will she remember, thirty years later, what she didn't want to remind herself of? Will it flood over her—watching him dance with someone else, being teased once too often when she wanted nothing more than to be noticed, his saying something, his saying nothing—whatever it was?

———

I open the pages to meet a woman younger than I can remember ever being. Her world so fresh there was no vocabulary for it. Or rather, there was a vocabulary that did not do justice to the wonder she was feeling. Who am I to talk about her purple prose? I like nothing better than to test language, to see how much it will bear.

I want to be sympathetic as I invent these stories from these fragments of text, these lifeless lists of things seen and done, seen and done, accounts of shipmates who come briefly to half-life, then slide back into the obscurity of abstraction. I want to be, but I am not. Because, in the end, her abstractions disappoint me. What is a "good sort"? What does it mean, "too good to be true"? What does my mother mean when she says something is "especially interesting" and then stops, midthought, without saying why?

But isn't this the nature of a diary? How could she be expected to know what will rise to consequence? Suppose Hitler had been more successful. My mother's diary would be the "before" that would have preceded a long "after." It would have shown us what we had lost—places and people and a point of view. Historians would pounce on her peripheral observations: the mention of a Jewish woman who was afraid on the ferry, the negro dancing with a white girl at a nightclub in Paris, the Germans who stood up and sang their national hymn. My mother's innocence would seem prophetic.

Who am I to judge? And yet I judge. I grant myself that right. This is more than the curiosity I might feel if I had found the book at a garage sale, picked it up for two dollars and been intrigued by the date or the colored pages of steamship funnels and house flags, the odd inscriptions in the back: 2 Ys U R, 2 Ys U B, I C U R, 2 Ys 4 Me. Then, I would read it aloud, laughing occasionally, almost awed by the guileless world it revealed. But this is my mother, and I want her to be more than she appears to be.

So I make my way through her diary alternately enchanted and repelled. Why is my own mother such a cliché? The eternal embarrassment of the child. My adolescent self at war with her late blooming. Yes, and more—because I was born in the "after," and my world did not contain her ingenuousness.

JUNE 30

We had to get up at 5:00 this morning to take the train. We carried away a picture of windmills dikes and canals. And an occasional wooden shoe and native costume. We have a wonderful room in Brussels—private bath and shower and everything fine. We saw the city—the Royal Palace, the diff. statues, the huge court of justice—or Low Court—and the collection of Wertz paintings (so weird and pessimistic—of oppression mostly huge but depressing.) We saw them making hand made lace, too.

I hate how thoroughly she reveals nothing. How everything is reduced to the plane of everything else. I almost warm up when she begins to talk about the paintings, but then she adds the lace, as though they were equally important in her mind. She has every right to like the lace as much as—well, more than—the paintings. In fact, I might have preferred it if she did. If something—anything—had become significant.

What I am saying is that I'm hungry for the shaping power of language to resurrect experience. That at the very least I want not diary but journal, with its sporadic reflections, its impulse to assess and analyze. I want what comes with introspection . . . that's it . . . I want her to have had an inner life. I have taken on the role of critic, come to haunt the pages of a young woman's naive diary. But look—I can't help it—see how interesting she becomes when she lets herself go:

JULY 17
The Italians come in groups to dances for Italian girls have to have their mothers along. Unless he cares a great deal for her & is engaged, he seldom brings her to a place like that. We were rushed for dances as soon as we arrived. They are all excellent dancers—and do they hold you tight. I danced with one Italian fellow whose name was Adriano. He had worked in an Italian Bank in N.Y. and could speak English well. He was so cute looking—we all thot he looked more American than Italian. Leanna acquired a Count, and Anne her Alfredo and so they & Adriano & I went for a ride. They urged to take us home and Mrs. Crawford, our hostess & chaperone, consented because we were together. They took us by the Coliseum, beautiful by moonlight, and on out to St. Paul's Cathedral. The others took a walk and Adriano & I stayed in the car and talked about New York and Rome, etc. and even love. He said he liked N.Y. because it was "so unusual." He was so cute when he said "beggar man, git you

git you." [a few words crossed out] *He laid his head on my shoulder & tried to sleep.* [more crossed out, two full lines, with dark, dark ink]

What happened that night? The most sensual moments, and she crosses them out! Who crosses out lines of a diary? And when? The ink is so dark—darker than the ink she had been using. It would appear this censorship came after the fact. A day? A year? No way of knowing, though surely it matters as I piece together the puzzle of what made her tick. What does happen to her when she sees this years later? Surely memory will help her pry beneath the ink to discern what I cannot, for the life of me, decipher.

We half made a date for the next night. He said he would come & if I could go, OK. I was skeptical & didn't act very enthusiastic. (Am sorry I didn't, for I was). 4 o'clock to bed.

There she is, she's had a night on the town. And then look what she does! She regrets her lack of daring. I want her to tell him she'll meet him tomorrow. She got away from Mrs. Crawford, for heaven's sake, and then she censors herself again. Adriano, why didn't you realize she was just being shy? Or was there something else behind her skepticism?

The next day, her predictable litany of sights: Coliseum, *Moses* by Michaelangelo, stairs "brot" over by mother of Constantine from Jerusalem, Appian Way, another church, the catacombs ("it would be terrible to be lost there"). I don't care what she saw. I care about whether she will do what I cannot for the life of me imagine her doing. Not in her tight buttoned collars. Her librarian shoes.

JUNE 18
Anne, Leanna & I all dressed up for our indefinite dates—& Alfredo came with a funny fellow for Leanna & no Adriano.

*I suppose I could have expected it but I was disappointed—for
he didn't seem that kind. Leanna wouldn't go as long as the
Count didn't come, so Anne went, & the rest of us took a car-
riage & went to the Casino. Somehow, the thrill was gone and
we didn't have nearly the fun we did the night before. I met
one nice fellow, big, from Los Angeles who was studying in
Rome & almost went to another place with him but was too
skeptical. They aren't to be trusted.* [a few words crossed out]
Wish I had—now.

There she goes again, second-guessing herself. Limiting her
experience. I'm afraid for her. Afraid she won't find the self she
so clearly is looking for. Isn't she too young to be this cautious?
I wish I could push her over the brink. Then she might have
understood me. I guess I'm glad that at least she knew enough
to protect her innocence. Still, I could wish that when she went
to see the "Follies Bourgere" (her spelling), she hadn't added *and
they were good—altho' I was a bit shocked at times.*

Frankly, I wish she didn't use "altho'" and "thot" and "tonite"
and "thru," even if they are convenient shortenings. They make
her seem superficial. Without them, she could easily step onto
the set of a movie—a novel by Henry James or E. M. Forster,
done by Merchant Ivory Productions. She could represent
America in the face of an old, sophisticated Europe. A decadent
Europe. She could be open and energetic and inventive. She
could be doomed to heartbreak.

Which brings us back to Trueheart.

I'm still on his trail. His presence is everywhere now, flitting
in and out of the pages, residing in what isn't said just as much
as what is there. Trueheart is behind Adriano. Or underneath.
Or in front of. Whatever the preposition, he's there.

JULY 31
Played deck tennis, shuffleboard & bridge all morning. I

learned that Trueheart is an adopted boy—that he is very much interested in architecture and a very hard worker. He has something of an artist's temperament—things get on his nerves. But he has a good mind and I have quite a bit of respect for him.

It's only just now that she learns this? She's known him for weeks. What did they tell each other, these people who danced and sang out into the night? I envy her something. I don't recall ever, not even once, thinking that the dance was all. The very *fact* of the song. I don't recall living in the present in such a way that the future was not hurtling heavily toward me, or the past bearing down with its crush of recollection.

No, I may not be completely sympathetic, but I envy her like mad. Too bad I can't leave her in relative peace, dancing on shipboard to the "blarey" old Victrola. She does not need me poking about in her private affairs. She does not need my judgment, not now, not while the moon is out and she is still young. And she *is* young. She is only twenty-three. My birth is ten, no, eleven long years away from this shipboard romance. She's young, yes, but not *that* young. It's not the youth, but—as I've said—the innocence. I was twenty-three when my first son was born.

Still, look at what she has done. She has worked her way up from the farm to this moment when she meets a young Englishwoman, Winifred, who sits at her table:

AUG. I

She's not pretty—but witty and a grand good sport. She has the cutest expressions—typically Eng., of course, "a blank nuisance, my frock," "some dame" (her unknown roommate), "I'm only country bumpkin," etc. She has just returned from Africa and is going independently to the States for a couple of mo's. She couldn't believe that Anne & I taught school & paid our way to Europe. She calls us "children." Her dad is sending her—lucky bumpkin.

I wish she could at least say "damn." Of course, the "blank" could have been "bloody"—should be "bloody," probably was "bloody"—though I suspect "bloody" wouldn't have meant anything to my mother. So "damn" it is. It's still my version. I'm still in charge. The dead lose jurisdiction over their meanings.

Okay, I have to face it. I have entered the one-way street of trying to know the past. Flat up against the boundaries of the finite. I'm lost in a futile attempt to find my long-dead mother. How can I expect to be successful? This was a woman who made up a code for her own night out, who crossed out her deepest (most revealing) sentiments. She was hiding from herself, so what makes me think that she can't hide from me, that her words will give themselves away? This was a woman who thought of bridge as *luck*.

———

Maybe it was better when the romance was hot and heavy in my mind. When fiction reared its frivolous head to populate the pages of my mother's journal. But I've gone too far to retreat into the might-have-been. That would be too easy. Now I want to know the Truth, with a capital *T*. I want to uncover the facts and piece them together until they add up to the woman who raised me. The woman who, after her house had been flooded, midnight water filling the rooms and leaving river silt in every crevice, simply came home, rolled up her sleeves, and began to scrub. The woman who, when I asked to go to my friend's house, responded with "but you had fun yesterday." The woman who sometimes sang in the car— "The Sweetheart of Sigma Chi." The template of my memories.

JULY 20
Train again—but a clean, comfortable one this time. Our gang was all together and we got into the most interesting discussions about everything—love, marriage, religion, duty, etc. but the greatest of these was love. We decided what kind of wives we would make, how many children we would have

and the kind of house we would have. Leanna would have a model house, artistic & well kept up. She was not intriguing but apparent. Laura & Glenna would fall in love heavily & be good, so good, to their families. Joan was the "long drape" type—would fall hard and perhaps wouldn't have children. Ruth would be happy because she was matter-of-fact, Eliz. would belong in a Colonial home by a tea table, the gracious hostess. Anne would mould herself to her husband but would keep him guessing. I was to be a cute little mother—my husband & I would be "good pals." A combination of the "ruffly curtains" and "long drape" type.

I remember ruffly curtains, but no long drapes. And she definitely was a "good pal" to my far-from-romantic father. I don't know if she was a cute little mother—she was a mother, how else was I to think of her?

Something was bothering her. How do I know? Well, there's the official H. M. Customs and Excise notice to passengers: what must be declared. It contains the usuals:

TOBACCO, CIGARS, CIGARETTES, SPIRITS, LIQUEURS, WINE, FIRE-ARMS, AMMUNITION, EXPLOSIVES

and, surprisingly, as though they were also to be expected: OPIUM, COCAINE, MORPHINE, HEROIN. Along with these, the list contains the technology of the times, caught, now, in antiquated terms, rendering it oddly innocent even as it hurtles us toward GPS, iPad, YouTube, Bluray, Kindle, and XTC:

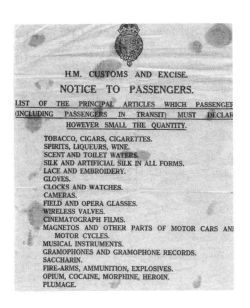

H.M. CUSTOMS AND EXCISE.
NOTICE TO PASSENGERS.
LIST OF THE PRINCIPAL ARTICLES WHICH PASSENGER (INCLUDING PASSENGERS IN TRANSIT) MUST DECLAR HOWEVER SMALL THE QUANTITY.

TOBACCO, CIGARS, CIGARETTES.
SPIRITS, LIQUEURS, WINE.
SCENT AND TOILET WATERS.
SILK AND ARTIFICIAL SILK IN ALL FORMS.
LACE AND EMBROIDERY.
GLOVES.
CLOCKS AND WATCHES.
CAMERAS.
FIELD AND OPERA GLASSES.
WIRELESS VALVES.
CINEMATOGRAPH FILMS.
MAGNETOS AND OTHER PARTS OF MOTOR CARS AN MOTOR CYCLES.
MUSICAL INSTRUMENTS.
GRAMOPHONES AND GRAMOPHONE RECORDS.
SACCHARIN.
FIRE-ARMS, AMMUNITION, EXPLOSIVES.
OPIUM, COCAINE, MORPHINE, HEROIN.
PLUMAGE.

And what do we do with the final item: PLUMAGE? Hats, boas? But this list was a part of her time and she had no reason to save it, save for what she had been scribbling in pencil on the back. Awful, oddball bits of verse, words cut off as though, in order to keep the whole, she has sacrificed some of its parts to the scissors that shaped it for her scrapbook. Scattered in all directions, the fruits of her mind as it searched for a rhyme, made a connection, tried so hard to be cheerful. Here, you don't have to take my word for it—see for yourself:

This girl called Glenna was a
sweet young thing—
to earn a living she could only
sing—
the [indecipherable] of this here tale
was that once she drank too
much ale
and the flirtation brot her a
diamond ring

Okay, so they were having fun. But then—there he is again, almost cut off the top of the sheet so that his name has lost its capitals:

> *A guy called trueheart*
> *play poker—*
> *And he didn't need to be*
> *joker—*
> *He'd bet & bet*
> *that Ann'd get set*
> *& if she didn't h*
> *choke*

Yes, they were having a good time, but some remark had bared its teeth, and these fragments, written up the page in the opposite direction, as though to counter the fun, are more than sheer coincidence:

> *they say you ain't got it*   *there was a person nam*
> *without it you won't make a hit*   *and everyone declared s*
> *w I maintain*   *quite a gal*
> *es there's a [indecipherable]*   *Her type they said*
> *es one thing you ain't got it*

> *Don't you let it, w*
> *For I know you'll*
> *And I*

She trails off . . . but it bothers her. She doesn't want to be that "type," the one who doesn't have "it," and yet, oh dear . . . I look again at the photograph taken on board the *Letitia*. Yes, the little row of buttons, the white collar and cuffs—I recognize something a bit prim, a tiny bit repressed. Something on the verge of disapproval. The other woman—the one whose hair spills into the wind—would suit me better, I think. The other woman, with the casual scarf and a careless air. But she remains nameless while my mother stares stolidly down at the deck.

So this is the subjective account—*my* version—of her version. I get to pick and choose. These are the parts of her diary that stand out—for good or for ill, but mostly for me. I will give them the meanings I want them to have. Some other daughter—the one she would have understood—would shape it differently. But these are the facts I have to learn to live with, or without. The "non" in nonfiction. The places where I delve into what is actually *there*.

Rome was one thing, Paris another. On July 25, 1930, someone shoved a note under a hotel room door and, voilá, in 2001, there it is in the scrapbook, waiting for receptive eyes. Real as can be.

The prettiest flowers of America have been transplanted in Europa gardens and they are the object of our loves With all our heart

I've had this yellowing scrapbook for years—brittle paper, pasted with menus and favors and ancient ticket stubs. Anonymous in the way that things out of context become artifact, not fact. I've had the photo album, and the journal. So why only now, seventy-some years after her tour, twenty-some years after her death, am I reading her into being? What is it in me that wants to find her now, when all those years I was content to leave her alone, stuck fast in the version she gave us? Yet here I am, sorting through all her sentences to find someone whose style I can admire.

JUNE 18 *We are acquiring the "Letitia Slant"—walking at an angle to keep balanced.*

JULY 2 *We nearly starved but Joan & I used our "will power" and didn't buy any cakes.*

JULY 4 *The Major got drunk and lay in the window boxes and everyone was disgusted.*

JULY 13   *Joan & I somehow failed to repress our mirth in Doge's Palace—and we didn't get properly impressed.*

JULY 15   *I never had so much fun talking languages mostly sign language.*

JULY 20   *We saw the Casino & roulette wheels & some gambling— which I didn't understand.*

JULY 22   *But there is no fun without some tragedy—and poor Elizabeth had cognac & champagne mixed and got badly befuddled. We got her home to her room, but she said the silliest things. She talked about "Bill" a lot and said "damn" much too frequently.*

JULY 23   *We saw Mona Lisa—and compared her to Joan.*

JULY 25   *Paris is a lovely place if you have money, but very tantalizing if you don't.*

JULY 31   *I'm getting bored with doing nothing. A life of leisure wouldn't appeal to me long—I don't believe. Too energetic to be satisfied that way. Oh yes, had my picture taken today.*

Wait. Had her picture taken? On the way home! All this time, I've been mistaken. From the outset, I've seen my mother setting forth in her practical shoes. And here she is, returning. This is who she has become *after* the transformation. I have to modify my preconceptions. Here's the list of purchases she made:

> *1 Scottish Plaid Shawl*
> *1 evening coat*
> *3 pr. suede gloves*
> *1 voile dress*
> *1 necklace (ivory)*
> *1 pack playing cards*
> *3 handkerchiefs*
> *etchings*
> *4 strings of beads*

No shoes. I could have sworn she would buy shoes that would help her hair fly loose. I could have sworn she would return with the feet of my other mother.

Okay, then. What else have I misunderstood? Here, in the scrapbook, the Cunard Line Passenger List.

Mr. L. A. Mark
Mrs. Mark
Mr. G. Marriott
Miss M. Marshall
Miss H. Martin
Miss L. May
Miss J. Meredith
Miss M. Merrill
Mr. L. S. Miles
Mrs. Miles
Miss Miller
Mrs. L. I. Mitchell
Miss A. L. Money
Miss Morrison
Mr. W. Mosby
Mr. J. A. Mulhall
Mrs. Mulhall
Miss M. E. Mulligan
Miss R. Mullins
Miss L. C. Murray
Miss V. Myers

Mr. J. Neilson
Miss S. S. Niccodemus
Miss B. Nicholoy
Miss M. Nichols
Miss R. E. Noble
Miss M. Noble
Miss R. Norris

Miss G. Obner
Mr. J. O'Hara
Mrs. O'Hara
Miss E. Owens
Miss R. Owens

Mr. C. D. Packard
Miss T. Parker
Mr. M. B. Parsons
Mrs. Parsons
Miss L. J. Pendell
Mr. T. G. Penon
Mr. J. F. Peterson
Mr. J. Petrie
Mrs. Petrie
Miss A. Pidcocke
Miss E. Pille
Miss M. C. Pipher
Mr. T. Poston
Miss M. Pratt
Miss E. Pray
Miss P. Prentiss
Miss E. Price
Miss E. B. Pritchard
Miss I. Prugh
Miss M. Publow
Miss M. Purey-Cust
Miss A. M. Putnam

Miss N. Radford
Miss L. L. Reilly
Miss Rencoast
Miss E. W. Renn
Miss D. Rice
Mrs. I. Richards
Miss O. Richards
Miss C. Riddle
Mrs. M. E. Ridout
Miss J. E. Ridout
Master R. E. Ridout
Mrs. M. Riley
Miss M. E. Riley
Miss A. Rissler
Miss H. E. Rolfe
Mr. W. G. Ross
Miss F. E. Rowe
Miss H. M. Rowe
Miss M. Rnssman

Miss F. P. Sadtler
Miss A. Sardam
Mr. W. R. Sattler
Mrs. Sattler
Miss E. Scherer
Miss D. Schram
Mrs. H. W. Scott
Miss G. E. Seegar
Miss E. B. Seegar
Miss A. H. Serkland

Miss D. L. Seybold
Miss F. I. Sharpe
Miss V. Shea
Miss M. A. Shea
Miss H. A. Shea
Mrs. D. M. Shearer
Miss E. L. Sheely
Mr. W. Sikkema
Mr. R. B. Silliman
Mrs. Silliman
Miss H. M. Simon
Miss C. Sims
Miss H. Slater
Mr. F. P. Smith
Mrs. Smith
Miss A. K. Smith
Mrs. M. Sonson
Miss E. M. Sotherland
Miss F. Southard
Miss S. Southard
Mrs. M. G. Spaulding
Mr. A. A. Spear
Miss G. M. Speers
Mrs. M. J. Stankard
Miss J. Steele
Miss F. Stoakley
Mr. Strifler
Miss W. A. Stuart
Miss M. Stuart
Miss L. L. Stuempel
Miss E. F. Sullivan
Miss M. Sullivan
Miss L. J. Sutton
Miss E. Swinehart

There she is—Tourist Third Cabin Passengers, Southampton to New York (via Havre), under *P*: Miss L. J. Pendell. Verification.

Let's look for Trueheart. Yes, under *T*, they list a "Miss Trueheart."

They must have it wrong. A typographical mistake. I know the group by now—I'll bet they teased him mercilessly. Still, the seed of doubt is sown. What if the other woman in the photo is Trueheart herself? Maybe T. H. is my other mother. Miss Trueheart, of the billowing skirt and sexy shoes.

No. I know my mother, I know the woman she became. Even if she did spend one evening fashioning an oddly unbreakable code, she would not write "he" in place of "she." She thinks nothing of saying how much she likes Anne, how she and Elizabeth adore each other. The women in this diary are vivid and real. Believe me, if Trueheart had been a woman, I'd know more of the story than I do.

So I return to her journal, to the cracking brown leather that sheds its papery flakes like ash whenever I open it. I turn again to the list of addresses in the back. On the page for *M* and *Mc* I find Ethel Bockler and Lucille Sutton. My mother has not been as precisely orderly as I assumed. He must be here somewhere.

Aha! Halfway down the page for *R* and *S*, I see: *Willis Mosby "(It.)"* The handwriting is tentative, and he gives his address as simply Lynchburg, VA. Beneath Willis, in an awkward, nearly illegible script: *Truehart Poston, Lynchburg, VA "(Art & poker & fighting)."*

This is a revelation. Trueheart was not his last name! Back to the passenger list. Tourist Third Cabin: Miss A. Pidcocke, Miss E. Pille, Miss M. C. Pipher, Mr. T. Poston. *Mr.* He exists!

Has he lost his allure, now that he's Poston? Now that his heart has lost an *e*? Only in the way that fact dulls the sheen of the possible. Makes it workaday. Oh Trueheart, my other father, I liked to think of your long line of heirs bearing your name into the future. I liked to think that—seventy years later—I might meet the sister I never had. Now you are lost. You are one more odd given name on a tombstone. One southern drawl turned crisp in a northern mouth. This is not your story, after all. Nor is it my mother's, although (altho) her voice wakes on the page, goes lively before it drifts into silence. Because hers was a "record," which is not the same thing as "story."

No, this is *my* story, the tale of how one day I tried to give my mother the romance I felt she hungered for. Posthumous romance, as though I could make up a life and hand it to her, and that alone would alter the direction of my own. But I'm too old for fantasy. In the end, I try to crack her code, its silent subterfuge. Something to do with drinking, a cemetery, and a wall (or a cemetery wall). It's pretty clear there was a speeding car, a dog, a doorbell. July 6, 12:20 (or is it 4:00) in the morning. Lucerne. I do not fully understand the tuxedos or the coat, though they are suggestive enough to make you wonder.

It has taken this long to get to the place where the journal trails off on its sad little note of optimism. Trueheart knew what he was talking about: life moves on. Soon after my mother got

home, her scrapbook sported new favors—a comb from the Victor Hugo Restaurant in Los Angeles, postcards and flyers from Pikes Peak, the Petrified Forest. My story, however, has a different ending. Yesterday, in the hope of seeing—really seeing— her, I sifted one last time through her photograph album. The one before the one with the baby pictures, the Greek-revival house, my father's familiar face. My mother in front of a cafe in Oberammergau, wearing, no, it isn't, but it might as well be, the same dress. A schoolteacher dress. Collar and cuffs.

There, glued tightly between "deck tennis" and "Glenna, a shipboard pal," right there he was, his name in her handwriting— Trueheart—where he had been all along, if I had known enough to know what I was looking for.

Each corner has been cut diagonally, indicating that the photo has probably been removed from one album and transferred to another—who knows how often? It has lasted all these years. Clearly, it survived the flood of 1946, and then another flood as well, in 1972, the wake of Hurricane Agnes. Carefully dried and replaced, a reminder of "before." But it's mine now, and I pry it loose from yellowing paper that tugs back. I force it from the shiny spots of glue that have held it in place for forty, fifty, sixty years; I leave bits of the backing behind.

He is dashing in his casual, crumpled collar, his dark good looks. He hooks his right thumb in his pocket, a half-smoked cigarette held nonchalantly between the fingers resting on his hip. He will go bald, that's clear, but his baldness, too, will be attractive. There's a tiny cleft in his chin. It's only later that I notice other details: wooden deck chairs; tuba-shaped air intake vents with their deep, hollow interiors; a curious rigging with pulleys and ropes; the floorboards striped with sunlight and shadow; some children in sandals spilling across the background to where it washes into white. Trueheart stares straight into the lens with modest self-assurance. His heart is true. He knows who he is.

Poston, you were wrong. You couldn't simply disappear like that, passport in hand. It wasn't ever going to be that easy. There was too much at stake. You must have known you would be called upon sometime, like now—because I would need you. I would need your logical arguments to remind me that this is the story of what I cannot do. I cannot change anything.

In the wake of Trueheart, my mother met my father. Or else there was no wake. He was a nice enough fellow, good for a laugh, but just not quite her type. A bit too unwilling to be "good pals," too much inclined to "fighting." Or maybe those ineffable moments that were "best left blank" were simply seasickness. Or, yes, she loved him just a little bit and her heart was slightly broken, but then she got over it, as people do. This much I know: somewhere on a train between Innsbruck and Venice, Trueheart taught my mother how to bet. Taught her the difference between a straight and a flush. The definition of a full house. He made a gambling woman out of her. When my father came along, she called it *luck*. The rest is mystery. The rest is hers.

The Same as Usual

My Dearest Lillian:

You will never *get so far away from home again I'm thinking if we can hold you back. it seems ages since we have heard from you but probably we* will *have a letter by the time you receive this. We received the one you mailed at Quebec. I had a letter from Mrs. Merril asking for the list of places you would be stopping at. I didn't have it either but yesterday she sent me this address so I would know where to write. Muriel Holcomb sent you a* nice box *of* candy *to the boat, and it didn't get there in time and she got it back yesterday, you ought to mail her a card from over there as she told me she hoped she would hear from you while you were gone. also Margaret Meeks told me Sunday she just* hoped *you could send her a* line *as she thought it would be* just grand *to* receive *a* letter *from Old Country, so do your duty, daughter.*

I know you girls must be having a fine time, How does Joan feel? was she sea sick? and were you? We are counting days to see you. Every thing here is the same as usual, we are making hay and with extra men and driving horses I am real busy. We are half through. Papa seems to be standing it pretty well.

We are expecting Geo's folks Sunday they will start for NY 2nd. Granda hasn't made up his mind to go for sure yet. Mrs Roberts is still there, she gets along with every body but Alice Williams she is to free to walk in and give her opinion. Pauline Gray is gaining slowly but *her father has Pneumonia and is very sick they don't think he will get well but he may fool them like Pauline has. No more news, and I hope we hear from you soon. with heaps of love*

  Mother & Father

A Study in Sunlight: Three Snapshots

The camera can only look backward . . .
—RICHARD RODRIGUEZ, Brown

THE HAIRSTYLES SAY mid-1930s; the daring array of skin says Europe. But it can't be. So I revise my idea of Puritan America, allow for the plunging backlines that reveal seven women sitting on the sand, facing (in varying degrees) the water that makes itself felt as a tiny line of horizon, only a shade darker than the sky. This is how they must have seen themselves, hip to hip in the dazzle of sun. Their hair, which ranges from dark to blond, has been pulled back into identical buns at the nape of the neck. Except for one, probably in a bathing cap, who looks almost bald in the lack of detail. High foreheads, not one pair of glasses among them. Hip to hip,

they glance to right and left as my mother steps back to make sure they are all in focus. Hip to hip, muses of sand. Though they are only eight. Eight young women gone to the beach.

The camera can only look backwards. Can only record the day, the year, the limitless stretch of water, the clear, fading sky. Can only tell us they were there—not quite posing for my mother's quick shot, but aware of her still, aware of the future lurking behind them. Caught in her little black box, a moment from which they would all soon depart.

Look at them in their not-yet-spandex suits, the fluid wrinkles of a fabric with a life of its own. See them looking sideways, maybe watching someone approaching, outside the frame. Could be a lifeguard, muscle and tan. Or it might be the ninth muse, late as usual, the one who is bringing sandwiches, thank god. The one with bright red hair unfettered in the wind. If my mother hurries, she can swing in her direction, catch her off guard. If she hurries, she can see her grow older, her wild red hair permed and parted, then graying, then gone. Snap. The shutter closes on all that light, holds it there in the darkness.

———

The camera can only look backwards, he says. Contaminate the landscape. Freeze the people in their two-dimensional poses. But the bear emerges from the woods in present tense, his shadow prowling before him. The bear's fur, the tufts of grass, even the dense thicket behind him, give off sparks. Partway up, the trees fade off into the overexposed flaw where light leaked in.

Still, he's there, a dark amorphous shape protruding from the woods, casting a sharper profile on the ground. His shadow will spill on down the embankment, protuberant snout leading him toward whatever it is he senses out in the open. Exposed and vulnerable.

Where did she stand in order to take this shot? She's probably in a car, window wound down, but I like to imagine her standing somewhere, in sunlight herself, glint in her glasses. The bear isn't looking in her direction. She stares at him through her one mechanical eye, as though what intervenes protects her. Maybe it does. Time is not lost, here. It could be yesterday. Tomorrow. In bear time, the sun vanishes. Night darkens and comes on. In bear time, the decades become one another. To date the photograph, one would look to the paper, the possible instrument, the techniques. One would never look to the bear, who might walk out of the woods right now and face you down. Who might turn away from you with your newfangled digital captivity. The trees are timeless. The grass springs back. On this hard earth he leaves no print.

———

Timeless, too, three Zuni children, lined up in steps in front of their adobe home. Beside them, a ladder catches the full force of the sun, white against gray, stairway to the sky. It cuts the photo into two scenes. In one, an empty bowl rests at the far right, at the base of the wall. Clay against clay. A cat curls, bowl-like, in the shade behind the ladder, hidden, or so it assumes, from our sight. A still life. Cat with bowl. And rising above them, the cracked wall with its promise of something else, something it would take a ladder to reach. In the other half, three children stare into the lens. You cannot see their eyes. In the background, an oven, hive-shaped, organic. Clay in which to fire the clay.

Sun beats on the ground, bleaches it white, spatters the sky with the leaves of the ocotillo. This photograph looks nowhere. It simply is. Children have stood there, stoic, for centuries.

So turn it over to see the past recorded in my mother's words: *Three little Mexicans in their adobe house (made of mud). We gave them pennies and they let us take their pictures—they could speak English—(on our way to Santa Fe).*

Suddenly a chasm of doubt. Surely we should take her word for it. The photo spells one thing, but she spells another. Once you ask questions, nothing makes sense. Surely she saw adobe— she defined it in parentheses. But these bricks seem so uneven, rocklike in their patterns, Mexican. Surely she heard English, but would Mexican children have had it at their command? Back then? For that matter, could the bowl be a basket? It leans so casually against the wall. The only certainty is the handful of pennies. Why would she mention them if they hadn't changed hands? The rest is open to debate.

In the long scheme of history, how could it matter? Let's say the children are our forgotten past, caught now in my mother's innocence. Let's agree that the picture speaks more than a thousand words, that words are fickle, subject to revision. That the past can be altered, resurrected, expunged. They stare back at us, the sun a sheen on the tops of their heads, the sun that bakes the skin brown, the sun that will walk the shadow of the ladder until it sends the cat searching for shelter, the sun that will ferret out the hollow of the bowl, revealing the patterns inside that could—if only they would—give us answers.

Sense of Play

ONCE MY FATHER TOLD ME he had had to decide which of two friends he would ask to marry him. They were each attractive young schoolteachers, each just a little too old to be still unmarried. He liked them both. On thinking, though, he had finally decided on the one with the greater sense of play. The story disturbed me, mostly because I did not recognize my mother in his final choice. I knew the other woman—my mother's first best friend, my aunt Peggy as I was allowed to call her, my "maiden aunt"—and she always seemed so carefree, so quick to laugh. Surely he meant it the other way around, that he'd chosen the one with the greater sense of responsibility.

Whenever I make an effort to picture my mother, she seems lost in the cloud of her circumstance: a voice calling us to dinner, the click of heels on the stair, sound of sheer efficiency. The years blend to one long chore. I remember her as tone. A chide. A disappointment. A silence at the core.

So imagine my surprise at the snapshot I've rescued from whatever obscurity it was enjoying between the green leather bindings of her album. Dead center, a young woman wearing a dark hat—not my mother, no, I've never seen *this* woman before—is sitting on what, under very close examination, appears to be a sled. There is no snow, or almost no snow, beneath the sled, although snow appears to be melting in patches on either side of it, dappling the ground. Behind her, three small trees—well, really just their slender trunks and a smattering of leaves—cut the vertical plane.

Leaves? Snow? It takes a minute to realize they do not belong together. An early snowfall, I would guess. October. Surprise snowfall, though behind the woman a white expanse with a line of tiny houses at its far edge suggests a small lake, or a very large pond. If so, the frozen stretch has welcomed snow. Maybe it's spring, April perhaps. All I know is that, against a background of bland white sky, the woman is wearing shirtsleeves, and doesn't appear to be cold.

First the eye is drawn to the objects she holds, the odd assortment of items piled around the sled—the pure thingyness of it all. Kettles and cooking tins with lids and round wire handles, large tins, the twelve-to-twenty-quart variety, and behind them a bucket or two. A blunt-ended shovel you can't quite call a spade, more like the kind to shovel coal. And a broom, angling up from behind like a fourth tree, a sturdy bundle of tightly bound twigs. She's holding a rope attached to something that looks like a bellows, but isn't. And there's something that might be a basket.

Then the anomaly: on her lap, a phonograph, the old-fashioned kind with a handle to wind it. It's open—you can see the needle resting on the middle of the platter, tipped a little on her lap. Or maybe not tipped, since the whole scene tips, and to straighten the sloping lake is nearly to topple her over.

Who is she, her hair hidden in her hat? Who is she on this warm, snow-struck day? What is she listening to? Her mouth is pursed and her eyes are slits. She closes her eyes in order to hear.

Or squints into the sun.

Now think of the time it took to amass the objects, to lug them to the edge of a lake one day in late October or early May. Who has time for such an elaborate ruse? It can't have been planned, because who could plan this snow littering the ground like a flock of pigeons?

And the music? It crosses the snow-covered pond, carried through icebound air. It picks its way through the long-lost elms, a tenor from Italy wafting through the tops of the trees, swooping in like starlings, then sticking around. She winds the handle, and it rises again, lifting raucous from branches to fill the sky. The snow recedes under its onslaught. It is summer in Italy, summer in his voice.

If she is working, what is she doing? If she is thinking, what are her thoughts? There is no context. I cannot separate work from thought. Why the shovel? The broom? Why, for heaven's sake, the phonograph? You can't quite call it a Victrola. Were they fooling around, fooling us, caught as we are, here in the twenty-first century? Did they postulate our presence? And who is this "they"?

Clearly she is not alone. No one in any photograph is alone. There is always someone on the other side of the lens. Someone who winds the film, who can ask her to move her foot, lift the handle, tip to the left so her head is caught between the two trees that lift from her shoulders like wings. Someone who receives the image, squints back in turn, thinking of the future. Thinking of the pleasure of puzzling us.

So the woman settles herself on the sled while her friend—fussing with angles, fiddling with the gear—arranges everything. She settles in to wait out time.

Looking at the objects, historians or dealers in collectibles might be able to tell the year with pinpoint precision, but I'm going to guess 1929—the year my mother's work was teaching high school in a small town in Michigan, the year after she had left the farm for good, but years before her work included husband, children, household tasks. My mother is free; maybe it's Halloween, maybe spring vacation, Easter Sunday looming and now all this snow to contend with. Hurry while it lasts. At any rate, they're giddy with freedom. And mischievous.

The camera is new, something my mother's new job allows her. Or it's borrowed, and before they return it, they think of one last pose. They'll show the photo to their colleagues, see how long it takes them to figure it out. They'll watch the men especially, watch their minds make a beeline for the facts. This is their conjecture: the women will circle around the image, burrow toward solution, but the men—they will either get it quickly, or not at all. In the end, this photograph is about two women, willing to go on a lark. Women who have impulsively suspended their work for one afternoon of pure, unadulterated fun. This riddle they've fashioned for us, their unsuspecting heirs. They go about gathering everything they can find that has a handle.

Or maybe they never think of us at all. Maybe they are simply acting, alive in the moment, making something to remember long after this day is over. Something to retrieve from lives filled with women's duties.

I see my mother alone at the sink, at the clothesline, making the beds. My mother running the vacuum, my mother ironing shirts—one after another, stiff on their hangers. Where is my father? Safely outdoors, doing what men do, which in his case was puttering in his garden—an inordinate amount of time spent for the asparagus and corn he produced. How much time does asparagus take? It pushes out of the ground each morning, phallic and ferocious. The next day you cut it—a clean, diagonal cut with the knife, near to the ground. When you're tired of asparagus, you simply don't cut it one day, and in a week it will reach out its feathery arms, a froth of green over the forgotten bed.

And how much for corn? After the initial nursing under inverted glass bowls, there's very little to do. You hardly need to hoe once the stalks have grown above the height of the weeds. Corn is simply a lesson in waiting. A lesson in sunlight and rainfall and fear of an early frost. It measures out the months, and when it is finally there—tassels bending in the breeze, yellow ear hidden inside its green jacket—summer is over.

My bet is that my father took himself outdoors in order to have the luxury of his own mind. Not the physicist's mind that the company bought and paid for, but his own sweet time to meander through what it was he thought of the world and his own life within it. He always looked as though he were working *and* thinking, and I suspect he rather carefully chose the vegetables that took the least work.

Fruit, as well. Just how hard is it to watch the raspberries move from green to red, to let apples suddenly appear, like finches, in the high branches?

The few times I went to my father's office, he was sitting with his feet on his desk, head tilted back, coffee cup balanced under its spiral of steam. *Working,* he said, though that did not seem like any work I recognized. *Thinking,* he said, as though the words were interchangeable.

If my mother was thinking as she ironed, she did not tell us and I have no idea what her thoughts might have been. Her mouth was pursed. Her eyes were slits. When I was older, she was insistent that I iron the collar first, though I have yet to see the sense in those instructions. If there were secret compartments in my mother, they were far too deep for us to penetrate.

You've seen it, though. You've seen the photograph: its amazing contrivance, its definite lightness of being, its seventy-some years of play.

So tell me, why am I so certain she was there? Is it because I recognize the results of her prodigious energy? Under the weight of that mountain of things, do I sense someone I never knew, but half suspected? The phonograph winds down, the tenor's voice slurs to distortion. Her sudden laughter fills the scene. She squints her nameless friend nearly into focus. In her invisibility, she is everything at once: ringleader, instigator, hidden director of the play. Offstage, she snaps one answer to her mystery.

4.

Always to link unknown things
to known things.

—JOSEPH JOUBERT, 1791

Certainty

1.

It is hard and round. Cylindrical.
It hides.

2.

Each morning the sun returns, now a little earlier than the day
before, noticeably earlier because we live so far north, so far west.
It rises in the east, from over the water, and it seems to carry with
it reflections of snow on the Cascades. Light falling, rather than
lifting. Tumbling down the hill that leads to the house.

3.

There are statistics.
Ask anything, there is an answer. An answer surrounded with if-
thens and buts, but nevertheless assertive, resolute.

4.

Each day you wake to its presence. You reach for the bottle of
pills that tell you it is there, somewhere beneath the outer skin
that was prodded and poked and cut and threaded. The skin
through which they insert a needle, which itself inserts the poi-
son that will kill what kills. If it kills what kills, which is what
they tell you is certain.

5.

Living with certainty can be interesting. It rounds the corner just
as you approach, leading you ever onward. You see nothing but
its back.

6.

Here's the rub. They know. They know so much. No question retains its rising inflection. The question mark is audibly erased. They tell you what you want to know, tell you they will always tell what you want to know. So what do you want, you who think you want to face truth? What actually is it that you want?

7.

The name becomes the problem. No one wants to hear the name. E-mails come with the subject heading: the dreaded c. But cancer, crablike, walks sideways into your life, and you must learn to say its name with the clarity it deserves. You must give it its due, its place in the lexicon. You must do that, not for yourself, but for others. So they can say it back. So they can roll it on their tongues, and taste its slightly acid aftertaste, its place in their lives as well. It's the one certain thing you can do for them—give this disease its living name.

8.

Outside, the clouds roll in. It will rain in the late afternoon. Or maybe they will pass, and the sun will spotlight the tips of sails on the sound. Flickers of light, triangular, as they lift like wings on this February day. You reserve the future, knowing that you will ride out into sun or rain, and that either will be fleeting.

9.

The long held note of the coyotes. Where do they live? We see their lit eyes in the headlights as they slink past, two of them trotting into the darkness, making their way to someplace close by. Over and over, they perforate the night.

We know they are there, but where—in daylight—do they hunker down? The morning dogs do not suddenly bark; their owners sweep up the hill tethered to leashes, and no one stops— looks around—fraught with the sense that coyotes are following.

No one halts, listening for footfalls, listening for what might be breathing in the underbrush.

10.

Here's what I know: the bamboo outside the window has grown another four inches over the past two months. It is resilient. Nothing cuts it back.

11.

There is no passion in certainty. Its color is tan, the color of sand stretching itself along the beach. Sand from a distance, uniform—not the multigrained reality it really is. This is the color of flax, or corn stubble. A nothing of a color, that persists and persists and persists.

12.

Arabic numerals, a pile of them, adding themselves, dozens upon dozens, incrementally growing by orders of ten. They march like soldiers across the page. Orderly. And punctual.

13.

Oh unlucky number, baker's dozen, oh, childhood lost to the start of it all. What would it take to return, to unbaby the body, harness the breast, become six again? Or seven, or eight? Boundless in your energy. Boundless, and bound.

Black cat, broken mirror, open umbrella. Spill of salt. Walk under a ladder, step on a crack, break your mother's back. Break your own heart. Break-dance your way out of the heart and into the head. Into the thick head of silence you will wish away and away and away. Flick of the switch. Wave of the wand. Wanderlust, lusterless, less is not more.

14.

Certainty sounds like a clock, chiming the quarter hours, adding its claim to the day. Each time, a little more, until the hour announces itself, passes on into the next, and then the next.

Certainty pulls out its card and places it, facedown, on the table.
Turn it over. It will be exactly what you imagined. It will contain
your exact specifications: name, address, phone number, date of
birth, social security number, counting out its digits as though
they could protect you, could put you back in place.

15.

The roots of your hair actively ache. The scalp is emerging as the
shape of your thoughts—round, and restless.

You did not expect to encounter yourself like this. The stark
expression. The round-eyed stare. The head that curves, baby
round, into the crook of your upraised arm.

Even as you surprise yourself in the mirror, you realize that
you recognize your head—its tidiness. You stare at your external
shape because, for the life of you, you cannot find the interior.
You have been turned inside out, vessel of attention, and only the
bones of emotions are left. You laugh in the face of your rubble.

16.

Not yet seven a.m., the streetlight still on, Sunday creeping
slowly up the hill. My dark window reflects back my books, lining the shelf of night. Soon light will seep into them, and they'll
tuck themselves away behind me. But for now, my books march
across my glass, left to right, pages of a lifetime. I keep only those
that have spoken to me, that made me what I've become. They
define me, now, as I've defined them.

17.

Each morning you forget. You touch the top of your head, and
you've forgotten. And you understand that when you remember,
you will have become a part of this disease. So you wake to for-
getfulness, grateful for the fact that nothing has diminished to
the point of memory. White cells. Check. Red cells. Check.
Markers. Check. Mark yourself checked in the mirror, checked
into the day, checked over, and under, and through.

18.

Lately, I never win anything on my Bingo scratch-off cards. I have been trying not to see this as an omen. Some sort of sign that luck has abandoned me. Where does the human mind go when it thinks this way? From what primordial need for explanation? What longing of the animal to understand the stars?

19.

Workmen are building a new addition to the house across the street. Every morning, a fleet of vans pulls up. Young men wrestle with 2 x 4s, dig and trim and pour concrete. A gable has been built on the ground—something they will hoist above the new bay window. You have to imagine light streaming in, and the outside world turning its head. What will they see that they haven't been seeing?

The doorway is new—a slice of pane at each side—so the house takes on a different guise. Wears itself well. They're saving the blossoming cherry that reaches, now, with slender fingers toward the door. "Wet black bough." But today faces do not appear along its length. Today, petals are merely petals, precursor of spring, predictor of time's mercurial intellect.

20.

One drop of rain at the tip of each leaf, suspended, certain. Cautiously held in check.

21.

There is a vocabulary and you learn it. Then you learn to forget it. Adriamycin. Cytoxan. Taxol. Taxotere. Tamoxifen. Arimidex. Everything has an x in it, as though you could solve its equation. There is a vocabulary, as well, for what people will say. Your blood pressure will rise as they tell you to "think positive thoughts." If thought could cure you, you would not be sick in the first place. You do not respond well to what seems to have become adage: hold a good image in your mind.

Yet you laugh. You are in an amazingly good mood. How can you not laugh at how you resemble a plant in the mirror? A dandelion gone to seed, to be precise.

How can you not laugh at how reasonably well you feel considering how you look? The images you hold dear (though, thank god, not the ocean under a blue sky that the social worker suggested) are positive enough:

Benjamin at the piano;

Simon dancing;

Ian running on the beach.

You have others, if you need to call them up:

Driving Route 2 across eastern Montana;

Through the telescope, your own young sons boarding the ferry across the estuary in Salcombe;

Stan on the merry-go-round, its carved horses handsome in sunlight.

But you don't call them up—not consciously. Not in the way they prescribe. To do that would buy their pronouncements, and you refuse to do that. You will not accept the blame that comes with failure to thrive. If you thrive, it will be willpower, and willingness, and, most of all, science. And luck. It will not be the day you gave him your love as the horse cast its wild eye backwards.

22.

Five a.m. Wake to darkness. Wake to its certain demise. Walk your thirty minutes, as though the lungs were what are at stake; as though to lunge into the day, sucking in breath and swimming upstream; as though to make seamless the dream of watery flight.

23.

This is hard work. Not only the body destroying itself, but the hard long wait for it to recover. The bones ache with all their silent activities. The mouth sheds its cloak and reveals every fissure. The only thing that actually tastes good is ice-cold water.

Beyond that are compromises you must make with the body. You must, after all, eat something . . .

24.

When it's gone, one thing is certain. I will not miss it. The breast that turned against me, against my will. It held lovers, and babies, but most of all it got in the way of things I wanted to do. To be. Soon I can try my new image. I can fit myself into the clothes I want to wear. Tailor myself. Talk myself into what I will become. Certainly, that will happen. My hair will grow, curl I hope, and my mouth will return to its normal contours. I'll catch a glimpse of myself in the mirror and say, "I know what you look like, underneath all the hair and the clothes and the faint brush of powder." I'll know what resides in that body I'm slowly getting used to.

Even the rain carries a different light. It slants into the house, harbinger. Everything is green, a haze of moss. Daffodils push through the ground. They are urgent and unsettled, the color of sunlight, caught for a brief instant through the storm.

25.

This puzzle will be the death of me. Three feet long, one foot high, it stretches across the table as though it knows it will defeat me. Oh, there's the requisite barn, dead center, some trees, a couple of cows, but mainly it's three feet by four inches of sunflowers, blowsy in the breeze, slightly out of focus in their frantic dancing. Hundreds of them. And three feet by three inches of variegated sky, the shades too subtle for the eye to discern until you've selected the wrong piece.

There is no ending. The pieces swim up in impossible progressions. The powers of concentration are overwhelmed. Is that the partial center of a sunflower, or part of the post in the obligatory fence? Is that stalk, or grass? In that sky shading off to the east is there a hint of darkness descending?

It's an American dream, made with German precision. The scene is so placid, static. You might think the whole of a lifetime was held in the frame, slowed to the point of contemplation. Yet when you step back, there the sunflowers are springing into a frenzy, twisting their sunbound heads, a sari of seed and petal and stalk.

Go inside the barn, where the faint smell of hay wafts down from the rafters, and the scent of manure is somehow clean and replete. It's dim inside, a summer afternoon held at bay, time for a thought, or, god forbid, an image. All those days ago when you entered the barns of your childhood, awed at the height, the heft of it all. When did you stop thinking of barns? Three summers ago, on an island in Quebec, you visited a dairy farm as though you were strange to its habits. As though you didn't know stanchion and hayfork and pail. The sweet smell of sileage. The soft sounds of cows shifting in unison. As though you didn't know that all of life is memory filed in the mind: been there, done that.

I know one thing. Three days, or three weeks, I can't predict the date, the hour, that I'll pick up the final piece and place it squarely where it belongs. But when I do, it will be almost mysterious the way everything will suddenly shimmy into resolution.

5.

We are poor passing facts
warned by that to give
each figure in the photograph
his living name.

—ROBERT LOWELL, "Epilogue"

On Snapshots: A Sonnet

Grandma, when did the world get color?

—SIMON, LOOKING THROUGH AN ALBUM

THIS IS NOT ART. This is the black and white of birthdays and summer vacations. Grandma's Sunday best. The telltale fading sepia, crimped white edges of the fifties, wavery Polaroid warping that tells us what era they're from. Here, in the album, I view each person or place as though I were the one

squinting into the lens. Someone is watching. And now I'm watching their watching, watching the hand as it steadies itself for the shutter-snap concentration. The shadows deepen and they hold you, caught in the primary colors of your time. Good eye, we say, when someone catches

that ephemeral instant and brings it to life. Soon the snapshot itself will be endangered. Stored on their slim silver disks, relatives will keep quietly to themselves. But how will we come across their oddball antics if we can't pick them up, shuffle and sort, then settle them back in their boxes on their cluttered

bottom shelf? How will we encounter the drama—the dullness and dailiness and deliberation—if we can't unearth them, give them their longed-for last chance?

Who

OH MY GOD, who is she? I want her for my own. I want her affinity with all those chickens, her lopsided leaning, her house all atilt. I want that tipping chimney and the angle of her neck as she lets one hen push its way into her heart, another pose as a hat. I want that practical dress and the long black stockings, even the sensible shoes. The light that fattens itself on late-afternoon windows, and the shadows that lengthen the yard. The chickens that peck at their shadows, whittling away at their lives. Look at the way light catches each shingle, each brick, each clapboard lining the side of the house. Look at it fasten itself to the folds of her skirt.

This was a moment—the day of the chickens. But all days were chickens, scattering feed, and gathering eggs. Off lens: the henhouse with its strange, musty odors. Off lens: the rustle of worry at the doorway, the nattering fuss as her fingers sift through straw. Chore after chore. The lifetime that added more, and then more.

I want this moment, but not what it stands for. Want one minute of overlapping shadow, one slapdash second of light. Quick, while she has a perch on pleasure. Quick, before her tiny breasts grow bigger, before she lifts up her hand to lift down that feathery weight.

Punctum

DRESSED AGAIN IN UNIFORM, he has made his way to Goodridge Brothers studio, cinched his belt, stiffened himself before the painted backdrop, drawn himself up to his full height of five feet two, and faced the photographer's prying eyes. Deep in his pose, he stares past us.

His name is Christian Wassermann, and if you go into the Visitor's Center at Appomattox, you will find him on their computer: Grand Army of the Republic, Ohio First Regiment, Light Artillery, Unit M. He'll be out of place—or rather, you'll be out of place, announcing to the friendly guide that you're looking for someone in the Union records. All heads will turn, and you will suddenly realize that what you had taken for granted—the side that stood for what was right—is still, in their eyes, wrong. That is the moment you will understand what it is to live in history.

The story is quick and easy. At seventeen, he came as an indentured servant from the streets of Hamburg to work on a farm in Ohio. Four months later, he was kicked by a mule and, determined to get as far away as possible, he ran off to join a German-speaking regiment. Soon he was marching through Tennessee. Irony haunts our family stories, and in this case, Uncle Christ was so small that his soldiering consisted of being assigned to drive the ammunition carts—often pulled by mules.

War is not civil. But it has its civilities. On Sunday mornings, my father's great-uncle would wake early and make his way to the nearest church. Families invited him home for dinner, where he would tell how hungry the troops were. Inevitably, he'd come back to camp with the remainder of the ham, and after that his fellow soldiers often woke him on Sundays, saying (or so the story goes), "Quick, get up, the ham bell's ringing." This, of course, must have taken place while they were still safely ensconced in the North, long before he made his way to Shiloh and Chickamauga. Long before he returned to a life of ordinary

routine—a life where each year he would dust off his uniform and attend the reunion, attaching one more ribbon to commemorate the days when he was most alive.

Here, where his right knee should be, there's a large white gash that appeared, most probably, more than fifty years later—after the flood of 1946. Peeling apart the sodden prints, my mother's hand was too quick, too urgent. A piece of my great-great-uncle stuck to the back of someone else, and nothing could be done but save what was left of him drying in the sunny backyard, the house itself still a sea of mud. What water can do! I remember. From five years old, I remember. It looked as though something had gotten loose inside, gone wild and dangerous, kicking at sideboards, lifting and toppling furniture, leaving a trail of destruction. Lucky Uncle Christ, that my mother thought he mattered when he easily might have been consigned to rubble, part of a past that has no market on despair.

Here's a digression: behind the scenes, the photograph carries a story of its own. The Goodridge Brothers—Glenalvin, Wallace, and William—came from York, Pennsylvania, to the Saginaw Valley in 1862. The first African American photographers in northern Michigan, they made themselves part of the community, even inviting Frederick Douglass to make a speech in 1868: "Give the black man the ballot; let him alone; and let him do for himself; let him work out the problem of his own redemption and elevation; faithfully make good to him the pledges which the nation's peril wrung from its slow justice . . ."

The Goodridge brothers adapted—daguerreotype to stereo-opticon, collodion glass negatives to film. Through their eyes, we see the city rise—its sawmills and lumber camps and fancy new hotels. Through their eyes, we see the water rise in the flood of 1904. See their reputations grow as justice makes good its slow word.

———

Another photo: the house after that flood, with the tree that came to rest in front of it, so that all that long summer my father and his friends worked with the two-handled saw to dismantle it, piece by piece, and then further to whittle it down, with an axe, to firewood. All the windows are open in hope of a cleansing breeze. Almost as though to taunt us, similar rough circles puncture the wide front porch, trailing off like puffs of smoke in front of the house my mother left so she would never have to live through a flood again. The damage to this photo almost certainly comes from the flood of 1972. Another time, another place, and still water found its way into the bottom drawers of memory.

The story is quick and easy. Absence holds our attention far more than the details that surround it. The eye moves to what is not there. I stare at the ragged perforations that spray the paper like gunshots, trying to penetrate the past. And they gaze back, with their flat white eyes, as though they could open the aperture on the present, look through each unplanned moment to where it slips into and out of significance. As though they could see me now, peering past my childhood home, piercing my great-great-uncle's unyielding knee, probing time's fluidity. From a second ruined living room, a second hellish need to wash away what is carried in the river's seething center, my mother wages her uncivil war. She cannot understand why an old man kept the promise a fierce young soldier made kneeling between those skittish flanks, why my father so gladly recounts a dapper white-haired man who, every Sunday morning, roused himself to go to Sunday school. She makes no fretful peace as she tugs at the pages of her life and they resist—leaving multiple wounds that will fester here in yet another century, record of what might be called regret, what might be legacy.

Downriver Construction Company

THE FLOOD ITSELF seems like a dream, a five-year-old's dream, where things swirl and mix. My father hoisting me onto his back in the dark of midnight, the water swirling and angry, reflecting nothing in the rainy night. And then water creeping through the grate of the hot-air register, water spilling out onto the floor. In the morning, a rowboat at the front door, and the water a sheen, almost calm, as it spreads itself over the landscape. Our house in the distance, where, two days later, my mother will set to work scouring the sediment that has settled in the teacups, washing the curtains and bedspreads, throwing away soggy carpet and warped drawers.

The huge tree ripped from somewhere miles upstream and left in our yard. The year it took to stack and dry the wood.

Gail (my father's boss), Bob (my father), and my yet-to-be-uncle Ray (just back from occupied Japan). All that seems so long ago, when they'd climb out of their old gray Chevrolet to help dismantle the tree. They sang and laughed and stopped to drink a beer or two while they sawed and sawed—handsaws, long two-handled crosscut saws—weekend after weekend until the tree was a pile of logs by the chicken coop. They fixed the tangled plumbing and built new cabinets to replace the ones they ripped out. Down to the studs, the house exposed, the smell of wet plaster and always the stale scent of silt, as though something feral had been set loose. And then the aroma of woodsmoke rising into winter air.

Where

HEAD-HIGH IN CORN. Surely that girl is me, so familiar the scene. I can hear it grow. Husks brush against the leaves, a bit like the sound of women's silk stockings, saved up for fancy occasions; the leaves click and mutter in the breeze and tassels wave their fingers. It could be me under that canopy, losing myself in those endless rows, scaring myself with the thought that I'll never find my way out. That I'll turn and turn under all that whispering, get lost in the shadows that snap at my feet.

The back of the photo says "Grandpa Lammert and Linda in Charles Cornfield on Aug 20—1946" and the writing looks suspiciously like my own grandmother's, but it could belong to someone else. There are no Lammerts in our family, and whoever Linda is, I've never heard of her. Still, there's an intimacy, even in such a short summation, because someone somewhere thinks that someone else knows Charles. Might even imagine the contours of this cornfield, or place it with pinpoint precision on a map.

It's 1946, the year after the war, and everyone is filled with a feeling that corn will grow taller and taller, now that the boys have come home. Surely Linda is five, like me, about to go off to kindergarten, like me. She even has my overalls. But she has a grandfather to stand there behind her, his straw hat measuring the harvest, while mine are not even a part of my memory— more legacy, or lore. I love the way he hitches his britches high on his waist and the way his shirt becomes part of the blazing sky. She'll never get lost.

Though I've lost her. That is, time has erased the moment she shared with a man who shared in her future. Expunged anyone who could help me find this unlikely twin, wherever life has taken her. *Linda, I'm here,* I call through the cornfields. *Here,* she echoes. *Over here,* I call. But the leaves lift emptily in air, and the sun keeps on humming over our far-flung heads. Somewhere my mother pulls my hair back tightly into my braids and sends me out the door. I could get lost, but I won't.

Unknown

THREE MEN ARE ALMOST LOST in the foreground. One cap and two hats, ties and vests. The young one—you can see his buoyant body—is my grandfather, Benjamin Pendell. Before I am born, he will fall from the haywagon, dead from a heart attack before he hits the ground. But here he is more alive than in those formal poses where he pulls himself up tall and stares stiffly into the lens. Here he's in his element. The man in the middle—who could he be?—is identified only with a question mark. The *x* of any equation. Anonymity only heightens his importance. On the right is my grandmother's father, John, this young Ben's father-in-law. There—can you see her?—behind him, a ghost of a face swallowed by trees. I think it's my mother's young mother—why isn't *she* named?—her features obscured by the fact that, to me, she has always been old. As I must appear to my own Benjamin, who's never seen me running giddy up the down escalator, never watched me toss his small father high over my head. And how long will it be before Ian will peer at my image, surprised at how young I once looked? Here one minute, gone the next. The clouds cast doubt on the day with their formless interrogation. Light leaks in on the left. Oh don't let me stop there pondering the infinite variables. Let me find myself in that field with these three men.

Mayme

I CAN'T FIND HER in the albums. She's never there. Oh, she hovers in the background, or floats at the edge of the frame, and sometimes you see the back of her head, her dark hair wound in a braid. Don't you know she's too busy for this? All the primping, the fuss of standing still. She has work to do: dishes to wash, or muffins to make, or floors that need sweeping. Chickens to feed. She's even too busy for her real name: the frivolous length of it—Mary Ellen, four syllables to trip out the tongue. She'll settle for Mayme: what the little ones called her as she hustled them off for school, she the mother now at thirteen, after their mother died of "quick consumption." She'll settle for what her life hands her. From horse & buggy to the car and the jet: the sky an outburst of sound. From the calm of her thoughts to radio and telephone. Number plee-us to dial tone. From the familiar cadence of the farm to this frantic factory where she sews collars and cuffs. Here she is, typed on the front of the book. Amalgamated Clothing Workers of America, 1937–1942: Mayme—it's official—but her last name's spelled wrong. Ledger No. 289: a stamp for each month to show she has paid all her dues.

What/Not

NOT WHAT IT IS, but what to make of it. Snowman wearing my grandfather's cap. It could be my great-aunt Gretta, his sister. There she is, wearing her stylish tucked-waist coat, building a snowman out of nothing, a featherweight of snow. So little snow that he's a ghost of a snowman, half leaf, half luster. We don't ask who the children are because we know there's no answer. No sound will travel down through the years. We have only the stillness of this day, when they woke to whiteness, woke to the hush of winter filtering through branches. What did she think, that pretty young  woman, waking in snowfall? Let's guess *November*. Let's guess *first snow of the season*. She slips quickly from the bed and worries at the laces of her boots. Already children are marring the perfection. Already they are building this brother of cold. She might as well join them. Might as well bring him a hat and christen him Ben. They'll shovel more snow to his torso, but they won't stop his melting later that day, won't stop his sagging into his features until he's nothing but density, nothing but dream.

"Not aunt Gretta." That's all it says on the back, so what are we to do with this? Someone knows only the negative. That's where this begins. Not only who she's not, but also, obviously, what she's not doing. A patchy layer of snow and a saucy young lady posed with her dog. Dog on a stool? What's that in her hand? No coat? There's nothing to make of this fancy but fancy. She's off to see the wizard, the wonderful . . . see, there is the house perched flat on the prairie, Toto perched fast on the stool, and Dorothy (since she's not Gretta) perched on the edge of adventure, holding the fading print of her song. The pump in the background folds itself into the cistern; the cistern withdraws into the water table of the plains; and the plains pull back from the sky as though they aspire to monotony. Denial is hers for the asking. Let her wave her baton at the future, filling us up with the lack of her name.

Portrait

THIS IS GRETTABELLE. Her curls flow into the folds of her dress and her dress folds into time. And time itself stands absolutely still while she asks absolutely nothing of us.

"Main Street, North Adams"

No DOUBT ABOUT IT—they're a pair. His black to her white, her back to his face. Above the slash of shirt, his mustache and his tie complete their perfect equal sign, while behind, her shadow chides. He hides his hands, hat shades his eyes. Her blouse and apron reflect glare. The porch is darkness at their feet. All afternoon her glasses stare. She waits for us to free her from the spidery noose that holds her place in history. 1919. We sense the way their lives have gone: first husband dead, and he with all his children grown. What do they have left to lose? The war is over on Main Street. His youngest son is home again; her daughters all have daughters now. He looks ahead, she turns away. Distance is a kind of dance—slow attrition of the days, a tyranny of undertone. Stance is all we have of them. The clapboard's horizontal plane cuts through the outline of their lives as they stand facing us across the intervening years, chance encounter that will fuse her rough pinked hem, his knot at ease, our own unbridled mysteries.

"The Triplets That Were Born to Mr. and Mrs. Warren Snyder"

—IN THE HANDWRITING OF MY GRANDMOTHER, MAYME

Old photos always make me want to know the rest of the story behind them. I think it's the faded black and white of them.

—CHERYL MERRILL, UPON SEEING THE PHOTO

MABEL   MAY   MAUD
NOVEMBER, 1903

Your given names date you as much as your dresses. Almost as much as those odd little bottles (they *must* be bottles—you can faintly see how the milk's found its level—maybe they're gravity-fed). Think of your mother with her oddly formal "Mrs.," the laundry (no Maytag) and feeding (no Gerbers), then laundry again. Think of the ironing! I hope she has help. I hope she has hope for your future. You'll still be at home when your older brothers enlist. And you'll still be around when they come marching home (if they do) from that war to end all wars. They'll never mention the trenches, or the stench of mustard gas. You'll be protected forever. One by one by one, you'll find someone to marry. Somewhere to settle down. But here you are, propped up in the foreground, your DNA showing long before science will learn how to unwind its yarn. Here you are tippling at the elixir. Taking for granted that things come in threes.

When

It wasn't even a country when
    Jonathan Pendell

> (b. 1748) m. Mary Povis (about 15 yrs. old)
> and moved to Dutchess County, NY.
> Enlisted in Rev. War as a private. Re-
> enlisted several times. 1832, granted a
> pension (said to have lived to 107 yrs. old).

It was a country when Jonathan's grandson
    David C.

> moved to Michigan in 1856. "They
> came across Lake Erie to Detroit
> where they put their few belongings on
> the cars and came to Jackson where
> their household goods were put on a
> wagon and drawn through the woods
> to Hillsdale County by an ox team."

It was a country when David's great-nephew
    Andrew Jackson Pendell

> (b 1857) married Sarah Elizabeth
> Triplett. "(It is her picture that hangs in
> our hall.)"

It was surely a country when Sarah's granddaughter, Lillian

> worked her way through college at the Hotel Top-in-a-bee. Chorus line of waitresses. She didn't think of it as hardship—but as a place where she might have some fun.

Or we could follow other branches back to when sometime after 1834, one

> Margaret McCormack Morrow Jamison

>> married a man named Mincer. "In our family she was known as Grandmother

Mincer. She had a tremendous influence on George, Margaret, and probably on Harry and Leslie—her grandchildren—since their father died while they were quite young. Grandma Mincer ran the farm."

and farther back when
Charles Morffort

"took a load of cheese to Cincinnati, took sick with yellow fever and died. His body could not be returned to his home. Rachel married Reuben Gee."

Everywhere—those flimsy onionskin copies, so many names scrawled out in script or battered out on ancient Underwoods— until the naming is all that we care about and we've lost the lives, the very hardships of those lives. The hard ships they boarded somewhere at Dover . . . from Baden . . . in countries whose singular names have been erased from maps, we can't quite remember when . . .

Overlay

EVERYTHING CONSPIRES toward anonymity: the long row of decking, the rail that cuts the sky like a second horizon, the clouds dispersing themselves as though the bleached sun had withdrawn its solace. It's there, though—because shadows angle back, reaching for a past already discarded.

One foot before the other, one eye on lookout, one heart turning away. Soon—two days, or ten, who knows—there will be a statue, or a promontory, an entry to what, now, is only a gap between the boot and the deck, a space revealed in the way the shadow fails to connect to its source

Loneliness. They are no strangers to the way the body can go numb while the mind travels on, the way travel distorts memory so that the traveler becomes someone new, someone washed clean of history. And history is their enemy. It sticks to them like leaches, leaving them weak and anemic. If they look back, they'll falter.

When they put down their feet on land, the world will not stop swaying. A tilting world, where words forsake them daily, whirling up in the air like a scattering of birds. So they face farther west, and they walk their way over a continent. Or ride the locomotives into the pulsing heart of the machine. They mutter the unfamiliar pronouns. They shorten their unwieldy names. They make their way into the future.

Perpendicular

S TUCK, WITHOUT A CAR, on the flattest land you've ever seen. Alone in the middle of nowhere, sticking out your thumb. The telephone lines stretch tight, a strand of voices reaching coast to coast. The highway follows its own white line where it wants to go. So this is a visual depiction of the word *median*. The photo would be amusing even if you didn't know him—but you do.

Okay, so once my brother George hitchhiked across the country, and someone caught him there, making his vertical statement on a horizontal world. Okay, so he turned it into a postcard he must have sent to his friends. But isn't it chance that had him wearing that light shirt and those jeans, pulling the sky and land downward across the road, as though to erase the very forces working against them? As though to hold him there, growing roots, even as his thumb points upward—and away.

Try giving the scene a geography: somewhere on the outskirts of Kremlin, Montana; Salem, South Dakota; Enterprise, Kansas. Hard to tell which. You'd need to ask the birds that perch on those wires, the ones that flew off, seconds ago. Or the willows that follow the river. Test the accents that span the continent. Test my brother's mettle as he heads east, or west, depending on where you imagine yourself standing as you raise the camera to your eye. This was long before he did it—moved west, I mean. Long before his knees gave out. He jumps up on the divider and becomes the dividend.

———

Plot the equation. He's the y axis, measuring out the rate of change against the steady rhythm of the waves. And there's the moment, somewhere partway along our time together, when chance raised its toast, plotted our angle of probability.

Just off camera, someone is handing my young first husband a beer, or rather, another beer. Or probably not handing, since he already has a beer, but reaching out, as though to click glasses. Or not reaching out, but casually gesturing, so that the bottle bursts, unplanned, into the periphery of the lens. What does it matter, now that chance has entered the frame? There will be a moment when we stop measuring the abscissa of time against the ordinate of years. Why not this day, so that when we plot the Cartesian coordinates, it will all end at this moment—in laughter?

Dark against dark, light against light—and yet the angles of his bent elbows departing from the perpendicular define his profile, everything suspended in the space between what can only be imagined, what can be known. And now we know. This is the meaning of the word *discrete*. The word *disparity*. The word *divergence*.

———

White to dark to gray, the mountains fold themselves into distance. And beyond them, sky. The silence of the snow is everywhere. Snow in the foreground, itself folded, plane upon plane. Everything conspires to draw the eye downward to where someone's figure delineates the contours of the land. Calls attention to what would otherwise be lost to us, the world spinning slowly toward nightfall, and a hush you can conjure deep inside yourself. Memorized stillness.

My grandmother's spidery scrawl on the back of the photo— "Robert on his skis"—and suddenly I am alert to the scene. My father fills the silence with a silence of his own. His face is featureless; it recedes into the hills; his hat becomes just one more snow-filled outcrop. Still, you can see that he gazes out at the sweep of cold, the countryside open before him. His skis whisper. He listens to the sound of his own passage.

It's almost impossible to remember that he is not alone, so lonely a figure he cuts across the landscape. He steadies himself against his planted poles. Behind him, two parallel saplings echo his stance. Do they mark a trail? Measure depth? Seems likely. Look hard. Birds are wheeling in that sunless sky, and before him the tiny tips of his skis curve up, defining the word *deflection*.

———

So where did it come from? Shaken loose from its past, the postcard holds secrets within its secrets. No clues as to who bought it. Or when. And certainly not why. Nothing written on its back to unlock its significance. Yet someone saved it—and for some reason. Someone packed it away with all the others—the grandmothers and cousins and aunts—in a box. The glacier swells and ripples like an animal, alive in its wrinkles and fissures. Three climbers lean into their ascent. Dark against light, they are both of and outside this breathing grotto of ice.

Nothing here is true. Everything tips and leans and totters. Zoom in. The men wear ties and vests and suit coats. Identical summer hats. They might be a trio of singers, hired to serenade visitors to the Alps. *Ueberschreitung des Rhonegletschers.* Transgression? The dictionary contains no good translation for what they are doing. In the foreground, earth throws up its rubble, reminder of forces they are not even pretending to conquer.

This is how we know the word *persistence*. It could be that my mother continued to savor her young woman's journey, or my father refused to give up a lingering dream. It could be the image itself, resisting the dustbin, going well over its limits. See the way the eye keeps readjusting, trying to hold it all still.

———

There's anonymous and then there's anonymous. How did she know she wouldn't be labeled, wouldn't define herself unless she stepped out of the album's depths? Somehow—just in case—

she's decided to give it her best for posterity, has put on her hat and positioned herself, a towering Tower of Pisa leaning over the straggling daisies she's clearly tied up so they won't all fall down.

This is the implication of *upright*—this straining away from the vertical. Everything—chimney and doorway, fencepost and lamppost—tilts to the left. The shadows drift right. I struggle to straighten them, as though I could steady my father's old Leica. Could hold her in its animate eye.

She's ready—standing there, sometime midcentury—hair pinned back, handbag and gloves, headed to church in those sensible heels with the cutout toes. Or on her way home, humming a hymn, the garden again an Eden of sorts. Whoever she may be, she's all suited up, waiting for me. And what am I to make of her, caught as I am in a time of my own? She's clearly not art. And not memory. She signifies absolutely nothing except that someone once put her dead center and let the angles right themselves around her living name.

Thingamajig

Y OU ONLY RECOGNIZE that distinct shape if you lived through the era of the 45 RPM. And we didn't know exactly what to call it, even then. Snap in that insert/adaptor/thingamajig. How do you re-view a generation? They say that old age robs you first of later memories, then of earlier ones, so I guess I'm stuck with the oldies (if not the goodies) even into senility. Stuck with Eisenhower in the White House and the Cold War in the world. *On the Waterfront* to *Gigi*, the first issue of *Playboy* to the Barbie doll, James Dean to Fidel Castro, the Lone Ranger to Rosa Parks, Stalin's death to the Edsel, Sputnik to the Peace Corps, the first golden McDonald's arch to the demise of the Burma Shave signs—you only get about half a decade's worth of involuntary memory. Five to seven years where just one note heard over half a century later will strike the chord of recollection. Mine spans "Mr. Sandman" to "Mack the Knife."

This morning it was not the tried and true, the *They asked me how I knew, my true love was true* kind of melody, but something all untried and probably untrue in a *next of kin to the wayward wind* kind of way, which is probably something anyone born post–*Let me hold your hand* does not recognize. But I do. Anytime the radio features an oldy-but-goody from the fifties (something they do not do so often now that the sixties and seventies are also old and good), I find that I know every word. Every single word. Which is testament to how often I let those records spin on the turntable as I teased out the indiscernible, so much so that, once I knew each word, I knew the song complete. *Oh! My pa-pa, to me he was so wonderful* and *First the tide rushes in, plants a kiss on the shore.* That kind of drivel—and it's all still there, still revolving in my brain.

Then, we were trapped in a vocabulary of romance. And a syntax. And I must say that those days before Orbison forced the high note of our solitude, even before Elvis lured us with his dusky *muh muh muh I get so lonely* or the flip side with its wail of *IIIII'll never know*—those days had a kind of magic. I suspect it came from all that repression for which the fifties are now famous, but those songs contained a sense of *I've hungered for your touch* that has now gone out of style. Now, people just touch. Then, they hungered. And we hungered along with them. Hungered at each and every sock hop in the high school gym. Each and every varsity basketball game where we sat, girls in one row, boys in another, paying as much attention to the other row as we did to the game itself. We spent hours on the phone assessing the results of these events. Did he? Didn't he?

Sometimes he did. He called and then you went bowling or to a movie, and sometimes in the dark there was a discreet reaching of his hand for yours. Or, if you were lucky, an arm casually draped along the back of the seat, a brush of fingers on your shoulder. That's another thing gone the way of vinyl: dating.

A date began with an invitation. A declaration of interest. It was formal. It could be recorded on the calendar, referred to as something first in the future, then in the past. There was an etiquette to follow: no kiss on the first date; or, if you cheated, you didn't say, and definitely a kiss on the second, or you knew there wouldn't be another. Then a tentative move toward more passion, what was called "necking." This happened at the drive-in movies, or listening to the radio in the backseats of old cars on the back roads out of town—usually on roads with the now-obsolete yellow sign that seemed, somehow, appropriately cautionary:

DEAD

STOP

END

Necking was essentially still just kissing, though it could begin to steam up the windows on cool evenings. That, in turn, carried with it the gentle fear—the almost-wanted thrill—of what was called "petting." Petting was what your mother did not want you to know about. Or do. But of course you did.

Those were the pre-pill, pre-abortion days, so you lived with the sense that you, too, could have to spend a year "living with your aunt in East Aurora," or, worse yet, might "have to get married," which happened all the time. You'd see your ex-schoolmate walking down the sidewalk pushing a stroller, sixteen years old and already out of commission. Your life and hers had diverged—just like that. You were locked forever on one side of the divide. Luck, you called it.

But there was something magical in a time when the words of the songs held longing and loneliness, not violence and cynicism. When they held out the promise that things could be fixed by time alone. *Time goes by so slowly, but time can do so much.*

We've lost other things we lived with then. The playmates dead before their time. The iron lung, now who could miss that? The summer I worked for Dr. Gutierrez, we heard the new Salk vaccine had just come in to the hospital and each doctor would be allowed ten doses. He tossed me the keys to his precious Lincoln and told me not to let it get scratched. I still drive those five miles with trepidation. I got there, only to find I needed the names and ages of the people he planned to vaccinate. "Just make them up," he told me over the phone. And I did.

Now kids lose their friends to drugs and suicide—not half as instructive as polio about how fate is sometimes simply fate. How indifferent and indiscriminating luck can be.

Gone, too, some of what we took for granted. The supper hour—that time when families sat down and ate together. The Sunday-evening Jack Benny shenanigans. The Ozzie and Harriet world. That gave way to "just the facts, ma'am," and, in perennially busy lives, food on the run. Of course innocence is not the only thing that's gone. And it wasn't even innocence, even then— it was the look of innocence. The look of what life was supposed to be—all lit up and tied with a bow—house and husband and small town ease. It was a sham, but we somehow wanted to buy into the deception, we wanted to make things better.

Is this nostalgia rearing its head? No, I think it's reflection knocking at the door. Wondering why those songs are so indelible. So full of schmaltz, yet also something genuine. Something *how-much-is-that-doggie-in-the-window* real. As *real as this feeling of make-believe.*

It wasn't all that long before that evening in Edinburgh when we—here, I mean "we," a group of university students— attended a party across from the local theater where the Beatles were coming to play. With lofty amusement, we looked down as the street filled with a crowd of teenage screamers. We didn't know a new generation had come, that we'd lost the right to judge. Despite our sophisticated scorn, we were forced to learn new words: *Tangerine trees and marmalade skies* and *take a sad world and make it better.*

And then—just like that—the sixties hit us full-blown. Our former classmates were fighting in Vietnam, and there was violence in our streets. The Beatles churned out another kind of schmaltz—*all you need is love*—and we had grown old enough to know better.

But all you do need is a kind of love when those tunes float up and rekindle whatever it is that makes you remember what surely you *want* to forget. I'm talking about those tunes that ought to be eminently forgettable. Do we really need *itsy bitsy teeny weeny yellow polka-dot bikini* or *white sport coat and a pink carnation* going through our heads all day? Do we really need to conjure that Friday night at the diner when Mary Agnes ordered a hamburger, then remembered what day it was, but decided to eat it anyway since Father Rogers would not want her to waste money? Meatless Friday has disappeared, yet we need to invoke it because we—here I mean "I"—need to remember Mary Agnes, whose father just died, fifty-four years after she did, still mourning the loss of his beautiful sixteen-year-old daughter in an accident she probably caused. Put these on the list: bench seats; no seat belts. *Memories are made of this:* Mary Agnes at the jukebox, belting out the words to songs she will never be in danger of losing because they are pure present tense.

Then summer turns to winter and the present disappears. And we—here I absolutely mean "I"—who escaped the fate of that tragic June night long enough to learn more slowly that her fate is ours, yet again hear the tight harmony of the Platters (*Deepening shadows gather splendor*) as swish . . . the spinning needle . . . swish . . . brushes away a lifetime . . . swish . . . a whole generation of lifetimes. Swish.

Why

ONIGHT, THE ROTOR WHIRRED so close, so loud, it spelled mayhem, spelled inferno, and then up and over the hill until it was a faint stutter of sound, far off, reminder, and I was spiraling down the flight of years, back, and back again to that tiny courtyard—Praça Pio Onze, Place of Pius the Eleventh. Pious place of calm within the storm.

Here you see only the dark doorway, tucked back and away from the entrance, and only later the stark blacks and sheer whites, the absence of shadow in equatorial light. White upon white upon white stretching into the distance, and the orange tiles of the rooftops drawn out in layers of glittering sunlight. Why, at the sound of one helicopter circling, did Rio return to me now?

It couldn't be sound that transported me here, where I have only to open the door to step into coolness. It couldn't be sound because all I remember is a steady whoosh of traffic, and a chatter of maids in the courtyard. The blue hush inside shuttered windows, everything muted, and mild. The popsicle vendors calling—*Kibon, Kibon*—on the beaches, and somewhere my own heart attuned to the lack of my tongue.

If it couldn't be sound, what was it? The briefly hectic sky—as though vultures were whirling above me, riding the thermals. Circling like kites in the effortless sky. Yes, maybe the light and its absolute absence of grayscale. Or the why were we willing to challenge ourselves in that climate? And the why I now call it a storm.

The panic, the daily rotor of panic. Daily the fear I was losing myself. Who senses the self in the ongoing order of things? It was there that I felt most American. Most aware of what shaped and sustained me. Most conscious of what I could lose.

So I look now at photos of family who packed up the words for *sausage* or *mittens*, tied them with string, and then put them away. I look now at people who managed what I couldn't handle. Why wasn't I made of their mettle? They turn away from my self-absorbed question. They have no time for my year of mute displacement. Necessity was a hurricane inside them. They had work to do, cows that needed milking, language that needed to be learned.

Haworth

If I pay the roots of the heather
Too close attention, they will invite me
To whiten my bones among them.

—SYLVIA PLATH, "Wuthering Heights"

BLEAK ON THE NORTH Yorkshire moors, the town waits out the century. Here you see only the white doorway of the tiny antique shop where I bought a pewter salt cellar for my mother. Everything else is some shade of gray. So still. Everything leads out and away. Walk down the dingy hillside, beyond the rain-slick cobbles, to where you can turn and look back at a town perched on the lip of oblivion. Walk into the haze of purple heather where the only sound is *curlew, curlew* and the heart grows wide and lonely. This is the interior land-scape—the one that mirrors language and contains the inner ear.

Imagine being whittled down to bone by consumption, staring out the confining window into that tiny churchyard where generations upon generations lie in absolute stillness under flat stone markers.

Millstone grit. Lying there on the couch, let your mind drift again onto the moors with their scattering of wayward sheep and a path that takes you over the faint trace of the Roman road that runs its straight line into history. Ridge after ridge as clouds sweep their strobe shadows across them until the moorland itself resembles the restless sea that will carry you westward, where a young woman you conjured in your feverish dreams hands my mother a gift.

Half in Shade

I'D SWEAR IT'S my mother—the woman whose face is a lamp—but the more I stare, the more she moves into the realm of uncertainty. And anyway, which one did I mean, the one in the doorway, obscured by the bulb, or the one sitting placidly under the shade? Here's what I recognize: the stance. The way she stands there with her arms crossed, a slit of forehead. So now, the other one puzzles me. Shirt or blouse? And who else is there, snapping the shot? Is this contrived, or improvised? I don't know a soul. So why not put him there, camera in hand? Or no, let's give him the starring role.

So there he is, wearing his lampshade, working on what I assume to be his thesis, something that keeps him up typing well into the night. Something that makes him prop the dictionary over the back of a chair and then lets the words float for a moment before they affix themselves to meaning.

Someone could probably date this photo and tell whether the person with no head is, or isn't, my father. Someone could tell me the make and year of this trusty black typewriter, make out the dates on the calendar, label the clock. But no matter how much I zoom in or out, everything stays out of focus. I can't tell whose picture he has pinned to the wall. If I could identify the person in the picture, then I could own or disown him. But what does it matter? I'll take him in.

I'll take night after night of his limning the edges of science, shedding this bare bulb of light on what he thinks it all means. And now it is time, so to speak, to put pen to paper, to let everything he's taken in spill out again like rice.

Chippa chippa chippa chippa-ta da-ding. Chippa chippa chippa chippa ta-dum-ding. The platen punctuates the silence. *Ding. Chippa chippa. Ding.* The clock spins its cycle of hours. Words slap on the beach of the paper like waves. His head swims with shadows of thought. He's about to shed light on it all.

By now he could be anyone, staring at these anonymous walls. He could know anything, locked in this room full of time. Come on. Come to bed. The world will be waiting. Come on— one last call.

But he will sit there until dawn comes spilling, whispering his insights onto the page. The chair will grow hard at his back, and his eyelids will droop, and then snap open. Beside him, the paper will pile up like snow.

It could be my father. It could be. But how would I know? Really know?

———

It starts with uncanny resem-
blance, but it's possible that only I
can see it—can see in their stilled
faces all I recognize of their living
presence. That would be wrong, of
course, since I never saw my father
in his three-year-old self. Yet I
could be sorting through a thousand photos and pull this one
out—that's him! Never, ever,
would I confuse him with his older
brother, my uncle Willy, who personifies action to the hilt.
Robert is taking in his brother's antics, absorbed in a way I have
known all my life: a quiet stepping back, a letting in, a making
of. His scientist self is forming, there in the wagon, posed with a
man I know I have never seen, not even in photographs. He's not
my grandfather, their father who, when I encounter him, exudes
a sepia warmth I swear is tactile.

This man's face is half in shade, and his sailor's cap cuts off
his hair, so all I can see is an older man who must (if I know my
grandmother as well as I think I do) be her father—Wilhelm,
the boys' Grandpa Schmidt. Not just because there's a resemblance to her—and there is—but because she would not let them
out of her strict sight unless it was someone she knew well
enough to trust with Willy's tendency to disappear at the turn of
a head. Which this alert man is *not* doing, not for a minute, as
he looks intently into the lens. Ah, but who's behind that lens?
Maybe she's carefully keeping an extra eye on those boys.

At any rate, aside from seeing my precociously pensive father
in his embroidered cap, I can't help noticing the way the wagon
wheels resemble those of the car their family is just about to buy
in 1915; the way my great-grandfather has carefully folded his
handkerchief and tucked it in his jacket pocket; and the way the
trees tip in the sky. I can't help seeing in my father's early face,

another face, a mirror image—the same engaged focus, the same inwardness directed at the world. Here he is, my grandson Simon—looking back at my young father, ten years beyond his death. I tell myself I might find this likeness anywhere, but I know that's not true, know the human brain learns early how to tell one person from another. Learns to identify. And

that's what I'm doing now: defining the limits of my stay. From the boy in the wagon to the one in my kitchen, a total of ninety-two years. Less than a century to stitch my life to the ones before me, the ones yet to come. Oh, I remember my great-grandmother counting my toes in German, so memory actually connects me back as far as 1853, but I'm talking about that physical sense of self within the other, that active belonging rising like sap in those spinning family trees.

How does the gene pool mix and mix again to throw up that one pure look of studied concentration? Eyes on the world. Oblivious. And in that look, my own oblivion.

———

Memory tosses in its sleep. The room is still. Half-light seeping in, gray morning, steeped in fog. Last night, light gathered at the seams of doorways and lingered there, a hush of light, once the eyes got used to the darkness. The kind of light no photograph can catch without the aperture kept open, letting it leak in slowly, like something learned by osmosis. What do we carry with us through a thousand nights, ten thousand nights—twenty-four thousand nights, to be exact—if not the memory of light? Anticipation of the morning's stippled silence. Day about to open its curtains and let us in.

Who stood in this very spot I recognize, and opened the shutter on my world? It might have been me, though I have no visceral feel of my body standing there, waiting for morning to yawn and stretch. But who else would know enough to love the way the fabric filtered sunlight until it turned you inside out? Who else would let light settle like dust motes,  flooding the floor with morning? And look, you'd think light had spilled on the film, but it's really the vertical streak (like retinal residue) where daylight worries at the corner, stands facing itself in the far window—the one you cannot see. I am the child at the bottom of the stairs. I know this scene too well—know all its shadings.

Yet clearly—there's the evidence—we do not have sole ownership of our remembered spaces. Now I see the vague shape of the cherry coffee table my mother bought sometime after I was married and gone—the one that floated during the last flood, then settled back, the books on its surface dry and open where she'd left them. Six feet of water on the first floor: I see the table shouldering its load, lifting it high. So this photo can be dated to somewhere between 1962 and 1972—a ten-year span for someone to usurp me.

Yes, this room bears an uncanny resemblance to habit: Christmas tree lights doubled, then tripled, in the panes of the double French doors; the animated chatter of my parents' parties as we lie above, looking down through the banister; the taste of popcorn and grape juice as we listen to *Our Miss Brooks* on the Sunday-evening Philco; clove scent of every vanished

Thanksgiving; the heft of a book in your lap and yourself a long way off, riding the moors, lost in the pages.

But someone else also loved the way the house admitted sound and light in equal measure until you could call out into glittering air, and hear it answer. Someone who immersed herself in the moment, the way Simon cups his hand so carefully over his toy grasshopper, the way his great-grandfather taps away at his evening, the way my own unknown great-grandfather slips himself so lately into my life under a rotary sky. The way the "greats" detach themselves, slipping gently from generation to generation until we—all of us—slip into half-shade and I simply cannot remember my mother holding so still, taking the morning in.

F-Stop

THERE ARE SEVERAL MOMENTS in her repertoire. Moments, shaken from continuity, that seem to reside in a tense of their own. Memory has always overtaken her with its intensities. And yet this particular memory seems to float free, simply to *be*.

She's about five, sometime before the flood of 1946, dressed in sweatshirt and oxfords, seated on the very top of a stepladder, her feet resting on the step below. Behind her, the sky, white and fathomless. Below, seated demurely by any standards, is her friend Gayle.

If they were playing dress-up, Gayle certainly got the best of the deal. She is wearing a long skirt and, over her shoulder, a colorful woven belt from South America. Gayle has had rheumatic fever and is newly allowed out of her house,

which is probably why she is sitting on the bottom step. Odd, though, because when she remembers the moment, she is always sitting on the bottom. Gayle towers above her, regal and pale, and she envies her illness, her vantage, her view.

This is the past, then, irrevocable, so why do I stick to her version? Already she's adjusting the f-stop to let in the light of revision. Already she's climbing that ladder to see what she saw, as though she won't mind if I lose her.

6.

And yet there were the intervals
that had to be filled in, the gaps . . .

—EDNA O'BRIEN, Night

Night Piece

Sometimes the things dreamers do seem incomprehensible to others, and the world wonders why dreamers do not see the way others do.

—QUEEN MARIE OF ROMANIA, AT THE DEDICATION OF THE UNFINISHED MARYHILL MUSEUM OF ART, 1926

EIGHTY-EIGHT BEAMS of radiation. I know, because I've counted, over and over, through the muted music as the machine hovers in one of its six positions, fixes in its open eye the place where my breast used to be, and beams. Eighty-eight . . . a full piano. A total of sixty to eighty gray (Gy). How interesting that radiation is measured in units of gray.

Every Tuesday, 3:00 p.m., I boarded the bus for the two-mile ride to take music lessons from Miss Curtis. She lived in a green Victorian with vast stone steps, a huge front porch, dark halls, and darker furniture. Murky, threadbare Persian rugs. The perfect house for an older woman called "Miss."

Every Tuesday, 3:45, there I was, sitting in the hallway, waiting for the girl before me to finish. The other girls were bigger, played better, didn't come from the tiny town where I lived. They knew something about music, I was sure, because they always seemed to open their books to things called *étude* or *nocturne*.

My book was not yet the elegant cream-colored affair I saw them using. Mine held pieces that could only be described as "songs"—and then, of course, there were all those scales. Part of me understood the nearly mathematical beauty of how the scales progressed, took on increments of sharps or flats, worked their way elegantly up the black-and-white staircase of the keys. Part of me thought that once you understood how they functioned, you shouldn't have to take that flight.

One Friday, right after radiation, my husband and I take a short trip south and east to the Columbia River gorge. Great river, swollen with water, rushing to the Pacific, its many rapids lost to a series of dams. And over the cleft of blue water, a series of bridges: Sam Hill Memorial Bridge, the Dalles Bridge, Bridge of the Gods. At night, streams of light mark the passage from Washington to Oregon.

The car winds down through miles of nothingness. Then, there it is: a full-scale replica of Stonehenge built by financier Samuel Hill, dedicated to the soldiers from Klickitat County who died in World War I. Perched high over the river, it seems somehow small, its clockwork perfection a diminishment. Each concrete "stone" traps the sky. It's hard, here, in the middle of this simulation, to imagine yourself standing in darkness while the sun lifts over the Heel Stone as though night had opened up along its seam.

Gently, almost religiously, I set the silk in motion,
and I saw that I had obtained undulations
of a character heretofore unknown.

—LOÏE FULLER, *Fifteen Years of a Dancer's Life,*
With Some Account of her Distinguished Friends

The total dose of radiation is fractionated (spread out over time). They tell me this allows normal cells time to recover, but what does that mean? Nothing is normal when you have a 75 percent chance of being alive in five years. And yet, each day I gain . . . if not confidence, then at least composure, as the lead rods wheel above me, start their syncopated whirr.

Miss Curtis herself was exactly what you would expect. Tall, thin, hair pulled back in a slapdash bun, tight line of lips, a pencil tucked behind one ear. It can't have been easy, a single woman in 1949 making a living for herself. It can't have been fun, haunting the rooms of that huge house, listening to its lonesome sighs. Its grand piano, blacker than the night. The pencil, it turned out, was for more than writing down the next week's assignment. It was for rapping your knuckles when your wrist dropped too low as you played. So, you worked your way up the keyboard, worrying about when the pencil might suddenly pronounce you deficient, devoid of any musical talent, undeserving of her pencil smile.

A mile from Stonehenge, on the banks of the Columbia, Sam Hill's Maryhill mansion rises out of yellow desert. Gilded, almost, like the Romanian furniture, a gift from his good friend, Queen Marie. In the basement, along with the cafeteria, are collections of a hundred chess sets, Indian artifacts, sculptures by Rodin. And one whole wall dedicated to art nouveau posters for Loïe Fuller's dance performances.

Loïe had dreams of her own. What girl from Fullersburg, Illinois, wouldn't have dreams? The silk whips itself into a frenzy. Diaphanous. What do we see as we watch "Night Winds"? Air made tangible. A twister from the plains of her childhood. Largo to allegro, she whirls then waits then whirls.

We cannot become accustomed to the idea that
we live in a world that is revealed to us
only in a restricted portion of its manifestations.

—MARIE CURIE, "Radium and Radioactivity"

I do not close my eyes in this thick-walled cave as the emissions sculpt the profile of my disease. If I hold myself still, the session is over in a blink. But think of Madame Curie working in her storeroom, naming the radium she laboriously whittled out of pitchblende, naming herself as she searched out the rays that might eventually spell my cure.

At home, my mother took up the challenge. First, there was the practicing. Up and down each scale, over and over, up then down, thumb tucked under, fingers curved, up then down, up then down, over and over. Forty-five minutes a day, rain or shine, friends outside while I worked my way along the length of the notes, wishing my way out into the light. When our mother went to the grocery store, I bargained with my brother for the amount of time we should pretend we had "practiced": twenty minutes for me, ten for him—that's about the best we could hope for. The store was only a block away, and she was only going for a "couple of things." The rest we would have to eke out somehow, rain or shine, friends or no friends.

Outside, day waited. I was a nine-year-old girl with a baseball glove and an ability to hit the ball. I was a nine-year-old girl who climbed trees and named herself Robert Bruce. Outside day waited, and inside I practiced the scales. I played my mother's dream.

On the upper floor of Maryhill, a black, low-ceilinged room. Three staged scenes, designed in 1946. Théâtre de la Mode. Here, several twenty-seven-inch models made of flexible black wire (once housed in the Louvre) strut the streets of Paris dressed in 1940s haute couture. Those tiny hats, mere whiffs of fabric. Little umbrellas. Strands of pearls. Miniature belts, petite handbags, diminutive high heels. Never in my life have I coveted those shoes—but oh, to be living in the age of those coats, their collars testament to wind!

And in the basement, tucked in a small glass box all its own, one plain scientific pamphlet donated by Fuller herself—and signed *Marie Curie.*

AMID NATURE'S

GREAT UNREST

HE SOUGHT REST

—SAM HILL'S SOLITARY TOMBSTONE

I become aware of my breath. Its shallow in-and-out, over and over. I listen to its intervals, its duration. I watch the wing-like flutterings on the screen as they mete out the range of exposure. Technicians come in to lift off what they call "superflab"—the rubbery mat they use to direct the diffusion. It fools the photons into thinking it is skin.

My own piano was the enemy. A polished burden of a beast on the far west wall. Light streaming in from the tall south windows. The sun came up and the sun went down; the piano stayed resolutely where it was, with its wide, triumphant grin.

I remember it as ever-present, but my parents must have bought it after we moved in, sometime after my seventh birthday. From before that, I can remember the room with its two sets of French doors, somehow tinier—cozier—without the piano's gloomy presence. I remember the colored lights of the Christmas tree, doubled and then tripled in the panes. I remember winter, white with pleasure, and the days drifting out, the yard a blank slate where our bootprints would sketch the maze for our intricate games of fox and geese.

I remember summer. Leaves keeping our secrets and the large back field echoing with argument: "Out." "No, safe." "No, out!" The apple branch broke while we were inching out on its length, and we rode it down like a storm. A flurry of whipped twigs, and my father's voice calling over them, "Are you damn kids all right?"

Who in Sam Hill was Sam Hill to have collected all these things? He's not the source of the saying—this burly industrialist builder of the first paved road in the Northwest, blustery seller of northwestern railroad bonds to European royalty, Quaker pacifist, and randy romancer whose illegitimate son carried his name while his daughter went mad and his son refused to speak to him—but he ought to be. And how did he collect all these people? Queens and sculptors and scientists, the dancer and the dance? Yeats had Loïe's image in his mind, yet an American businessman named Samuel Hill also kept her spirit alive.

The body is not bruised to pleasure soul.

—WILLIAM BUTLER YEATS, "Among School Children"

Two months after the night of the Recital, I quit piano lessons. Not easily—Miss Curtis did not make it easy, my mother did not make it easy—but indeed I finally quit. Whatever other girls might come after me, I could feel their knuckles cringe under the pencil, but I did not care. Let *them* learn how to quit. Let them learn that kind of courage.

The desert calls up something clear, and incontrovertible. The summer I turned fourteen, I spent two weeks in New Mexico, Arizona, and Colorado, doing what the Girl Scouts called archaeology. At Canyon de Chelly I dug up some potsherds, ones I only now realize were probably Anasazi, along with some kernels of burned corn—nothing notable, but still . . .

I hiked through Mesa Verde, descended ladders into the false night of the kivas, then up again into light. I looked out over land so flat that I could see what others must have seen before me: the short span of life any one person is given.

Loïe of such motion died of breast cancer in Paris at the age of sixty-five; Marie of such dedication died of leukemia, probably caused by the very elements she had discovered. And Sam Hill? He collapsed on his way to address the Oregon legislature, of something called "stomach influenza." He's buried on the bank below his Stonehenge. Across the river, the massive mystery of Mt. Hood fractures the sky.

I hear the girl she was. She's practicing. She's getting ready for the Recital, the one where she made the mistake that made her want to quit for good, that told her nothing would turn her into the musician she didn't want to become. She, too, has collected things. Baskets and marbles and glass paperweights. Russian lacquered boxes, a red wooden apple with three tiny cups inside. On the windowsill, there's a yellow porcelain piano, complete with tiny keys and a china music book, black upon white, waiting as if for her return. When you lift the hand-painted lid, you see a fragile box, holding a fraction of what she hoped to be.

Why measure time in days, when night will do? I overhear her metronomic droning, her calibrated dreams. She does not indulge the dark. Instead, she listens for the music of words, the way they clang and clatter, or fit smoothly into each other with an echo of consonant, an ease of vowel. She listens for the tempo of the mind. In the artificial daylight of the radiation room, she listens past the mechanical thrum of Muzak to count the pulses of the beams. She eavesdrops on the future, where she hears the high piping voices of children calling over snowbanks, winding their way through a circular maze where the fox cannot leap the blue shadows. Where they are, for the moment, safe.

Photographs Identified

The following notes provide further information and/or identification of the photographs included in this book; many still remain unidentified.

Paris: 1938; Classroom with Landscape; In Half:
My father's sister, Margaret Elizabeth Randels Warner, b. 1914, Alma, MI. In the early 1940s, Margaret worked with the American Friends Service Committee in Ecuador and Guatemala.

"With Cloud Chamber"; "Robert, At About 3 Years Of Age"; Plaid:
My father, Robert B. Randels, b. 1911, Alma, MI. Physicist with Corning Glass Works, Westinghouse Corp.

"Robert, At About 3 Years Of Age"; Circa 1873:
My paternal great-grandmother, Christina Ries Schmidt, b. 1853 near Buffalo, NY, and her sister Margaret Ries (Tante Maggie).

Great-Uncle Carl; Double Exposure:
The man referred to as "Uncle Carl" is Carl Schmidt, brother of my grandmother, Elizabeth. His childhood shoe is now the property of the Smithsonian Museum.

Where They Came From, Where They Went:
The people in the initial photo are unknown; Karl Schmidt, Langensteinbach, Germany, with wife and son, dated 1937.

Plaid:
My grandmother, Elizabeth Schmidt Randels, b. 1882, Saginaw, MI. In 1906 she spent a year in Germany with her new husband, George B. Randels, while he studied philosophy.

Classroom with Landscape:
Margaret Randels; Robert Randels; Martha Heetel and husband. The Randels family (George, Elizabeth, William, Robert, Margaret) spent 1926–27 in Freiburg im Breisgau, Germany, while George was on sabbatical, studying under Husserl; Martha Heetel became Margaret's lifelong friend.

Standard Time:
Photograph is of unknown men from the co camp, taken at our home on the River Road in South Corning, NY.

Girls in White Dresses; Parentheses; Trueheart:
My mother, Lillian J. Pendell Randels, b. 1907, North Adams, MI. Teacher of Latin and English.

Who:
The girl in this snapshot has been tentatively identified as Muriel Schambaugh, a neighbor of my mother's in North Adams, MI.

Punctum:
Christian Wasserman, b. in Germany, emigrated to the United States circa 1860, served in the Grand Army of the Republic, Ohio First Regiment, Light Artillery, Unit M; married Lizzie Ries from Buffalo, NY.

Downriver Construction Company:
My uncle, Dr. Raymond M. Warner from Barberton, OH, husband of my aunt, Margaret Randels; my father, Bob; their boss at Corning Glass Works, Dr. Gail Smith.

Unknown:
My maternal grandfather, John Benjamin Pendell, b. 1879; my maternal great-grandfather, John French Duguid, b. 1851; and ?, North Adams, MI; my grandmother, Mary Ellen (Mayme) Duguid Pendell, b. 1883, Ray, IN; Benjamin Cameron Kitchen, b. 2002, Seattle, WA; Ian Edward Kitchen, b. 2005, Seattle, WA.

Portrait:
My maternal grandfather's sister, Grettabelle Pendell Combs.

"Main Street, North Adams":
My maternal great-grandfather, Mr. and Mrs. John French Duguid—she is his second wife, Francelia Shepard.

When:
My maternal great-grandmother, Sarah Triplett Pendell, b. 1862, North Adams, MI, wife of Andrew Jackson Pendell; waitresses at Hotel Top-in-a-bee, 1927.

Perpendicular:
My brother, George Duguid Randels, b. 1943, Corning, NY; Andrew Thornton Kitchen, b. 1940, Leeds, Yorkshire, England; my father, Bob, others unknown.

Why:
Praca Pio II, off Rua Jardim Botanico, Rio de Janeiro, where I lived with my husband and two young sons, 1970 and 1971.

Half in Shade:
My father and his brother William with my paternal great-grandfather, Wilhelm (William) Schmidt, b. 1850, Langensteinbach, Baden, Germany, who emigrated to the United States in 1868; Simon Vincent Kitchen, b. 2003, Seattle, WA.

F-Stop:
Judith Randels Kitchen at age five; her friend, Gayle Armistead.

Credits/Notes/Serendipities

CREDITS ⟋

The photograph in "Rain Coming from a Bright Sky" is reprinted with permission from the United States Holocaust Memorial Museum. The views or opinions expressed in this book, and the context in which the images are used, do not necessarily reflect the views or policy of, nor imply approval or endorsement by, the United States Holocaust Memorial Museum.

The images of Loïe Fuller in "Night Piece" are all in the public domain.

All other photographs, letters, and documents are from family albums and archives.

NOTES ⟋

After I had published "Classroom with Landscape," I found evidence that Martha Heetel had sent at least one postcard to Margaret marked with a swastika, and that her husband had gone off to war and never returned, probably lost on the Russian front. She was reported to have "never fully recovered" from his loss.

The three sections of "Bits and Pieces" were taken from fragments of an incomplete manuscript written on the backs of scientific reports by Robert B. Randels sometime before 1980.

Further research into the origins of "Trueheart" yielded the following:

In 1934, Martha Eskridge Lee, a descendant of the Duke family in Virginia, married a man named Harrison Trueheart Poston. Built in 1939, Saint Mary's chapel at Chatham Hall, designed in the Jacobean Revival style by architects Joseph E. Fauber, Jr. and H. Trueheart Poston of Lynchburg, Virginia, contains stained glass windows depicting figures from the Bible and Christian tradition. No *e* in his heart, but yes it has to be him. In a cloudy photo, Martha—already caught up in Southern society expectations—seems a sharper carbon copy of my mother's softer pose.

An undamaged photograph of Christian Wasserman (identical to the one in "Punctum") is part of the collection of the Historical Society of Saginaw County and was featured in an exhibit of the work of the Goodridge Brothers for the Michigan Historical Museum. The digression (middle section) was written after the essay was originally published, when this information came to light. The fascinating history of the photographers can be found at:

www.hal.state.mi.us/mhc/museum/explore/
museums/hismus/special/goodridg/

Click on "Take a Closer Look." The archivists confirm that they had labeled that particular photograph "Uncle Christ(ian?)," so it's possible the identification came from someone for whom he was an uncle—my grand-mother, or one of her three children.

In researching the life of my grandmother for "Mayme," I discovered an "auto-biography" written in 1953 by seventy-one-year-old Bertha Wells Duguid, who was married to Mayme's brother, Dennis. She gives a good sense of the times: "We had to get water from the town pump, or go into Mrs. Belcher's kitchen, which was a bother to her. We had no stationary tubs or drains. We had a washing machine that was swung by hand. I boiled the white clothes and took all day to wash when there was a baby to care for, and feed. Please remember that there were kerosene lamps, wood or coal ranges, outdoor toilets, no run-ning water, no telephone, no radio and no television."

I have recently seen another photograph of the strange infant bottles found in "The Triplets That Were Born to Mr. and Mrs. Warren Snyder." A somewhat disturbing image of one is included in *Wisconsin Death Trip* by Michael Lesy, University of New Mexico Press, 1973, making it clear they were in use in the Midwest by the late 1880s.

The Maryhill Museum of Art in rural Washington State, which is the focus of "Night Piece," was founded by American businessman Samuel Hill along with Queen Marie of Romania and Loïe Fuller, the American dancer who took Paris by storm. The museum has permanent exhibits about her career. In his poem "Nineteen Hundred and Nineteen," William Butler Yeats paid tribute to Fuller's "Chinese dancers."

The initial photograph in "Where They Came From, Where They Went" is not part of my family's collection but did actually appear on my disk, as if by magic, when I picked it up at the camera store where my photos were being scanned. I've adopted its subjects as part of my history.

After completing "Double Exposure," I began experimenting with what could be done on the computer to enlarge a photograph. By narrowing my focus and zooming in several times, I was still unable to read the labels on the bottles, but I could make out other details: wedding rings, the designs on the pressed-tin ceiling, the folding extension of the phone's mouthpiece, feathers on the woman's hat, a woman's reflection in the glass of the door of the phone booth. Behind her, the wavery reflection of the street outside, with—probably unseen by even the photographer—a ghostly figure peering in. There is no telling how the imagination understands what is beyond the capacity of the human eye, but there he is—my unknown young man in his shirt and tie.

Acknowledgments

"Standard Time" (originally published in GREAT RIVER REVIEW) appeared in a slightly different form in DISTANCE AND DIRECTION, Coffee House Press, 2001.

"Certainty" (originally published in GREAT RIVER REVIEW) was awarded a Pushcart Prize and appeared in PUSHCART XXXVI, 2012.

Grateful appreciation to the editors of the magazines in which most of these essays originally appeared:

BREVITY
"On the Farm" ("Who" and "Where")

COLORADO REVIEW
"Sense of Play"

DEFUNCT
"Thingamajig"

THE GEORGIA REVIEW
"Night Piece"; "True Heart" ("Some of Lillian's Friends from North Adams—Note Car," "Girls in White Dresses," "Parentheses," and "Trueheart"); "The Speed of Light" ("The Speed of Light," "Half in Shade," "Punctum," "Perpendicular," and "What/Not")

GREAT RIVER REVIEW
"Certainty"; "Young Woman on Fence," "Robert At About 3 Years Of Age," "A Study in Sunlight: Three Snapshots"; "Album" ("Mayme," "The Triplets That Were Born to Mr. and Mrs. Warren Snyder," "Main Street, North Adams," "With Cloud Chamber," "Plaid," "Uncle Carl," and "Double Exposure")

ORGANICA
"Paris: 1938"

PRAIRIE SCHOONER
"Where They Came From, Where They Went," "Classroom
with Landscape," and "Rain Coming from a Bright Sky"

TRIQUARTERLY ONLINE
"Uncertainty"

WACCAMAW
"Overlay," "Why," and "Haworth"

This book received loving attention from everyone at Coffee House Press, and
I would like to thank them all. Allan Kornblum's astute editorial eye made a
complex project possible.

I would like to thank the skilled and compassionate doctors who treated me
over the past two years: Dr. Rebecca Corley, Dr. Jay Lawrence, Dr. Dennis
Willerford, Dr. Berit Madsen, and especially Dr. Bruce Stowe. Thanks—to
Fleda Brown, Mary Clearman Blew, Jennifer Culkin, Sandra Swinburne, Sheila
Bender, Cheryl Merrill for valuable suggestions; to Mitzi Hazard, for conversa-
tion; to Linda Bierds for believing in this form; to Dinah Lenney, for enthusiasm; to Kent Meyers, reader extraordinaire; to my sons William and
Matthew—these photos are in your keeping now; to my brother George for
helping me jettison the excess; and to Stan, the one certainty.

COLOPHON

Half in Shade was designed at Coffee House Press,
in the historic Grain Belt Brewery's Bottling House near downtown
Minneapolis. The text is set in Caslon.

FUNDER ACKNOWLEDGMENT

Coffee House Press is an independent nonprofit literary publisher. Our books
are made possible through the generous support of grants and gifts from many
foundations, corporate giving programs, state and federal support, and through
donations from individuals who believe in the transformational power of literature. Coffee House Press receives major operating support from the Bush
Foundation, the Jerome Foundation, the McKnight Foundation, from Target,
and in part by a grant provided by the Minnesota State Arts Board through an
appropriation by the Minnesota State Legislature from the State's general fund
and its arts and cultural heritage fund with money from the vote of the people
of Minnesota on November 4, 2008. Support for this title was received from
the National Endowment for the Arts, a federal agency. Coffee House also
receives support from: several anonymous donors; Elmer L. and Eleanor J.
Andersen Foundation; Suzanne Allen; Around Town Literary Media Guides;
Patricia Beithon; Bill Berkson; the James L. and Nancy J. Bildner Foundation;
the E. Thomas Binger and Rebecca Rand Fund of the Minneapolis
Foundation; the Patrick and Aimee Butler Family Foundation; Ruth and
Bruce Dayton; Dorsey & Whitney, LLP; Mary Ebert and Paul Stembler;
Fredrikson & Byron, P.A.; Sally French; Jennifer Haugh; Anselm Hollo and
Jane Dalrymple-Hollo; Jeffrey Hom; Carl and Heidi Horsch; Stephen and
Isabel Keating; the Kenneth Koch Literary Estate; the Lenfestey Family
Foundation; Ethan J. Litman; Carol and Aaron Mack; Mary McDermid; Sjur
Midness and Briar Andresen; the Rehael Fund of the Minneapolis
Foundation; Deborah Reynolds; Schwegman, Lundberg & Woessner, P.A.;
John Sjoberg; David Smith; Kiki Smith; Mary Strand and Tom Fraser; Jeffrey
Sugerman; Patricia Tilton; the Archie D. & Bertha H. Walker Foundation; Stu
Wilson and Mel Barker; the Woessner Freeman Family Foundation; Margaret
and Angus Wurtele; and many other generous individual donors.

To you and our many readers across the country,
we send our thanks for your continuing support.

Good books are brewing at coffeehousepress.org

MISSION

The mission of Coffee House Press is to publish exciting, vital, and enduring authors of our time; to delight and inspire readers; to contribute to the cultural life of our community; and to enrich our literary heritage. By building on the best traditions of publishing and the book arts, we produce books that celebrate imagination, innovation in the craft of writing, and the many authentic voices of the American experience.

VISION

LITERATURE. We will promote literature as a vital art form, helping to redefine its role in contemporary life. We will publish authors whose groundbreaking work helps shape the direction of 21st-century literature.

WRITERS. We will foster the careers of our writers by making long-term commitments to their work, allowing them to take risks in form and content.

READERS. Readers of books we publish will experience new perspectives and an expanding intellectual landscape.

PUBLISHING. We will be leaders in developing a sustainable 21st-century model of independent literary publishing, pushing the boundaries of content, form, editing, audience development, and book technologies.

VALUES
Innovation and excellence in all activities

Diversity of people, ideas, and products

Advancing literary knowledge

Community through embracing many cultures

Ethical and highly professional management and governance practices

Join us in our mission at coffeehousepress.org

JUDITH KITCHEN is the award-winning author and editor of several works of fiction, nonfiction, and poetry. Her work has won the Lillian Fairchild Award, a Pushcart Prize, and the S. Mariella Gable Award. She has served as judge for the AWP Nonfiction Award, the Pushcart Prize in poetry, the Oregon Book Award, and the Bush Foundation fellowships, among others. The recipient of a National Endowment for the Arts fellowship, Kitchen lives in Port Townsend, Washington, and serves on the faculty and as codirector of the Rainier Writing Workshop at Pacific Lutheran University.